The Channels of Monetary Effects
on Interest Rates

NATIONAL BUREAU
OF ECONOMIC RESEARCH

NUMBER
97
GENERAL SERIES

V

The Channels
of Monetary Effects
on Interest Rates

PHILLIP CAGAN
Columbia University

NATIONAL BUREAU OF ECONOMIC RESEARCH
New York 1972

Distributed by
Columbia University Press
New York and London

Relation of the Directors to the Work and Publications
of the National Bureau of Economic Research

1. The object of the National Bureau of Economic Research is to ascertain and to present to the public important economic facts and their interpretation in a scientific and impartial manner. The Board of Directors is charged with the responsibility of ensuring that the work of the National Bureau is carried on in strict conformity with this object.

2. The President of the National Bureau shall submit to the Board of Directors, or to its Executive Committee, for their formal adoption all specific proposals for research to be instituted.

3. No research report shall be published until the President shall have submitted to each member of the Board the manuscript proposed for publication, and such information as will, in his opinion and in the opinion of the author, serve to determine the suitability of the report for publication in accordance with the principles of the National Bureau. Each manuscript shall contain a summary drawing attention to the nature and treatment of the problem studied, the character of the data and their utilization in the report, and the main conclusions reached.

4. For each manuscript so submitted, a special committee of the Board shall be appointed by majority agreement of the President and Vice Presidents (or by the Executive Committee in case of inability to decide on the part of the President and Vice Presidents), consisting of three directors selected as nearly as may be one from each general division of the Board. The names of the special manuscript committee shall be stated to each Director when the manuscript is submitted to him. It shall be the duty of each member of the special manuscript committee to read the manuscript. If each member of the manuscript committee signifies his approval within thirty days of the transmittal of the manuscript, the report may be published. If at the end of that period any member of the manuscript committee withholds his approval, the President shall then notify each member of the Board, requesting approval or disapproval of publication, and thirty days additional shall be granted for this purpose. The manuscript shall then not be published unless at least a majority of the entire Board who shall have voted on the proposal within the time fixed for the receipt of votes shall have approved.

5. No manuscript may be published, though approved by each member of the special manuscript committee, until forty-five days have elapsed from the transmittal of the report in manuscript form. The interval is allowed for the receipt of any memorandum of dissent or reservation, together with a brief statement of his reasons, that any member may wish to express; and such memorandum of dissent or reservation shall be published with the manuscript if he so desires. Publication does not, however, imply that each member of the Board has read the manuscript, or that either members of the Board in general or the special committee have passed on its validity in every detail.

6. Publications of the National Bureau issued for informational purposes concerning the work of the Bureau and its staff, or issued to inform the public of activities of Bureau staff, and volumes issued as a result of various conferences involving the National Bureau shall contain a specific disclaimer noting that such publication has not passed through the normal review procedures required in this resolution. The Executive Committee of the Board is charged with review of all such publications from time to time to ensure that they do not take on the character of formal research reports of the National Bureau, requiring formal Board approval.

7. Unless otherwise determined by the Board or exempted by the terms of paragraph 6, a copy of this resolution shall be printed in each National Bureau publication.

(Resolution adopted October 25, 1926, and revised February 6, 1933,
February 24, 1941, and April 20, 1968)

To John, Laird, and David

Contents

Tables

Charts

Figures

Preface

[T]he paper currency in common use, being a currency provided by bankers, is all issued in the way of loans, except the part employed in the purchase of gold and silver. The same operation, therefore, which adds to the currency also adds to the loans: the whole increase of currency in the first instance swells the loan market. Considered as an addition to loans it tends to lower interest.

John Stuart Mill, *Principles of Political Economy*, New York, Kelley, 1961, p. 646 (in the original 6th edition, 1865)

Mill's explanation of monetary effects on interest rates, with its emphasis on bank loans, could be duplicated many times from earlier and later writers down to the present time. It is part of the tradition of monetary theory. Yet it has many points of conflict with other well-established theories of money. The present book is a theoretical and empirical analysis of the points of conflict.

This study originated in my earlier work on interest rates, in which examination of their historical movements revealed a significant inverse association with the rate of change of the money stock. This was not a surprising result, but it had not been analyzed statistically before. The association was shown to reflect a short-run monetary influence on interest rates. The ability to measure this relationship opened up the opportunity of testing the two reigning theories of how money affects interest rates in the short run. These two are the credit and the quantity theories of money, the former stressing the first-round effects of money creation through credit expansion and the latter stressing portfolio adjustments by the public to a change in its money balances. The test involves dividing monetary growth into two parts, one representing credit expansion and the other representing all remaining sources of monetary growth. A multiple regression then determines the contribution of each part to the total effect of monetary growth on interest rates.

Most of the statistical results came first, and to interpret them the theoretical analysis was done later. The results are not favorable to Mill's view, expressed above, and support instead the quantity theory. The two theories have important but conflicting implications for the proper conduct of monetary policy.

An earlier version of the statistical results of Chapters 4 and 5 was circulated in 1966 and elicited many helpful comments. I am most indebted to Milton Friedman, who encouraged me to expand the work and made many suggestions for improving it. A National Bureau staff reading committee consisting of Friedman, Robert Lipsey, H. Laurence Miller, and Anna J. Schwartz was also extremely beneficial. I wish to thank the members of the directors' reading committee, Francis M. Boddy, Maurice W. Lee, and Robert V. Roosa.

Parts of three other chapters have been previously published. Revised versions are presented here. Chapter 3 appeared in the *Review of Economics and Statistics,* August 1966, and was reprinted as *National Bureau Occasional Paper 100.* Chapter 6 was presented at a Brown University conference on monetary growth models and was subsequently published in the *Journal of Money, Credit, and Banking,* May 1969. I am grateful for the comments of the conference discussants of that paper, Carl Christ and James Tobin. The results of the first part of Chapter 7 were presented in collaboration with Arthur Gandolfi at the 1968 meetings of the American Economic Association and published in its *Proceedings,* May 1969.

Indispensable computational assistance was rendered at various stages of the study by Josephine Trubek Crouse, Jae Won Lee, and Irene Abramson. Martha T. Jones of the National Bureau's data processing department was continually helpful.

The text was greatly improved by the careful editing of Ester Moskowitz. The charts were expertly drawn by H. Irving Forman.

This study was financed by a grant from the Life Insurance Association of America, and their assistance is gratefully acknowledged. Their concurrence with the results is not to be assumed.

1

Introduction

THREE MONETARY EFFECTS ON INTEREST RATES

One of the oldest tenets of Wall Street is that tight money increases interest rates and easy money reduces them. Indeed, the level of rates is often taken to indicate whether monetary conditions are tight or easy. In that respect the connection seems tautological, but the considerable statistical evidence supporting such a connection is not based on a tautology.

Actually, in traditional theory there are three different kinds of monetary effect on interest rates — a portfolio effect, a credit effect, and an inflation effect. All three could be at work together. Their relative importance, however, is crucial to the theory of monetary dynamics. This study is concerned mainly with the first two, but the third one also comes in for attention at certain points.

1. The *portfolio effect* occurs because money and other financial assets are substitutable forms of wealth holding. A change in the rate of growth of the money stock produces a discrepancy between actual and desired money balances. This leads to accommodating changes in the demand for other financial assets and in their prices. The resulting changes in interest rates tend to remove the discrepancy, because these changes affect the demand for money balances and work to bring the amount demanded into equality with the changed supply.

When the rate of growth of the money supply changes, the growth rates of actual and desired balances continue (for a time) to be unequal. For as long as it persists, the discrepancy continues to affect interest rates.

Continued growth in the money stock does not, however, lead to lower and lower interest rates. A decline in interest rates stimulates investment expenditures. This raises aggregate expenditures and income and thus increases the demand for money balances. The economy gradually adjusts to a rise in monetary growth through a corresponding increase in the growth rate of expenditures and nominal income. In this process the initial period of falling interest rates comes to an end and the rates move back toward their original levels. Eventually a new long-run equilibrium is attained which, compared with the initial position, has higher rates of growth of money and of nominal expenditures and income and the same *real* rate of interest.[1]

The portfolio effect focuses on the substitutions that people make between money and asset holdings when actual and desired balances are not equal. To measure that effect here, the empirical analysis relates the level of interest rates to the rate of change of the money stock. The dependence of interest rates on monetary growth should be clearly distinguished from a relationship between the demand for real money balances and interest rates. The latter "liquidity preference relation," as Keynes termed it, shares a common parentage with the portfolio effect. The substitutability between money and financial assets lies behind both.

The demand for money balances depends upon the level of interest rates and other scale variables such as wealth and income. This demand takes part in determining the equilibrium relationship between stocks of money and other assets. The portfolio effect, by contrast, involves a dynamic adjustment sequence; it describes the effect on interest rates over time as portfolios are brought into equilibrium. The value of the interest elasticity of demand for money balances in equilibrium is not crucial to that adjustment sequence, so long as the elasticity is not zero (implying no substitutability) or infinite (giving rise to a liquidity "trap"). The crucial parameter for the portfolio effect

[1] There are two well-known conditions for the real rate of interest to be the same in the long run: that the initial position be one of full employment (otherwise the monetary expansion produces an increase in real income which, by the usual assumption, permanently increases saving more than it permanently increases investment and so reduces interest rates), and that redistributions of wealth resulting from unanticipated increases in the price level have negligible effects on the demand and supply of real loanable funds.

is the rate of adjustment to changes in monetary growth. The empirical relationships implied by the portfolio effect are not the same as those implied by the demand function for money balances.

2. According to the *credit theory,* an expansion of bank credit has a permanent effect on interest rates, unlike the portfolio effect. In the credit theory, money created by banks goes first into financial markets and adds to the total supply of real loanable funds,[2] which affects the equilibrium amount of borrowing and lending in the economy. To be sure, once the new money is spent by borrowers, it becomes part of the circulating media, supporting a higher level of aggregate expenditures and prices; thus, after the first round of its issue, the new money will be used in the same way as the previously existing stock of money. So long as the flow of new money continues, however, interest rates supposedly remain lower. Moreover, the decline in rates is not dependent upon lags in prices or other variables. If all prices rise immediately and proportionately to the increase in the money stock, money expenditures depreciate in the same proportion, and the continuing expansion of credit still augments loanable funds in real terms and reduces interest rates. The expansion is not solely in nominal terms, therefore, but also shifts the allocation of real aggregate expenditures.

It seems appropriate to attribute the credit effect, among modern writers, to Knut Wicksell.[3] He introduced the concept of the "natural rate of interest." At this rate the demand for loanable funds equals the amount supplied by current saving out of income. The natural rate can differ from the rate prevailing in the market so long as there are additions to loanable funds from money creation (or from reductions in desired real money balances).

Wicksell was interested in explaining how increases in investment demand produce inflation through an induced expansion of the money

---

[2] The concept of "loanable funds" here is all-inclusive and is meant to be the flow of funds or credit (I use the terms interchangeably) appropriate to the determination of the general level of interest rates in the economy. The sale of one nonmonetary asset to purchase another – portfolio swaps – is excluded. Only *net* purchases of financial claims by each person or business are included; such purchases can be financed by income receipts, net reductions in money balances, or the creation of new money.

[3] *Interest and Prices,* London, Macmillan, 1936 (originally published 1898), and *Lectures on Political Economy,* Vol. II, London, Macmillan, 1935 (originally published 1906).

supply. A greater demand for capital induces banks to expand loans if reserves are sufficient; by this behavior banks accommodate the money supply to the demand for bank loans.[4] Although autonomous changes in the money stock (such as those produced by gold flows) did not receive his main attention, his line of reasoning can be extended to include the proposition, set forth above, that creating money through an expansion of credit (given the demand schedule for capital) reduces interest rates.

3. In an analysis of interest rates it is important to distinguish between nominal and real rates of interest. Changes in the rate of monetary growth produce corresponding changes over the long run in the rate of price increase, and nominal rates of interest tend to compensate for anticipated changes in the real value of fixed-dollar assets. Increases in the commodity price level, for example, depreciate the real value of bonds, and the dollar coupon rate of new bond issues tends to rise to keep the anticipated real rate of return on the bond the same as it would have been had the actual and the expected price level remained constant.

The difference between nominal and real rates of interest was stressed by Irving Fisher as part of his theory of fluctuations in investment.[5] The distinction is relevant here because the portfolio and credit effects pertain to the real rate of interest, not to nominal market rates. An increase in the monetary growth rate, if it persists, will increase the rate of change of prices and, eventually, anticipations of that rate. By Fisher's theory, an increase in the anticipated rate of price change will raise nominal interest rates commensurately. In such a situation the

[4] Wicksell expected most changes in the money supply to be accompanied by such shifts in loan demand. If bank loan rates adjust only partially to the shift in loan demand, these rates and the money stock will tend to move in the same direction. This was given as an explanation of the "Gibson Paradox," a positive association observed between interest rates and the commodity price level. See the discussion in my *Determinants and Effects of Changes in the Stock of Money, 1875–1960*, New York, National Bureau of Economic Research, 1965, Chap. 6.

[5] Irving Fisher, "Appreciation and Interest," *Publications of the American Economic Association*, 1896; *The Theory of Interest*, New York, Macmillan, 1930; and "Our Unstable Dollar and the So-Called Business Cycle," *Journal of the American Statistical Association*, June 1925, pp. 170–202.

portfolio and credit effects will reduce real, but not necessarily nominal, interest rates.[6]

These three monetary effects on interest rates represent different adjustments of the economy to a change in monetary growth. The *portfolio effect* concerns adjustments by the public when changes in the money supply create a discrepancy between actual and desired balances. It does not matter how the new money enters the economy. The discrepancy leads to substitutions between money and other assets with repercussions on interest rates. The *credit effect* draws attention to the first round of money creation. This effect is based on the behavior of banks and the initial impact of their credit expansion on financial markets. Not only does money matter here, but how it enters, whether via lending or via direct purchases of goods and services, also matters. The *Fisher theory* asserts that an increase in monetary growth will raise nominal interest rates, once the monetary expansion leads to price increases and anticipations of inflation.

This study deals with the theoretical basis and empirical importance of these theories, and how best to describe the channels of monetary effects on interest rates. In many monetary theories and studies great importance is attached to the credit effect of money but without an explicit examination of the empirical significance of this effect.

OUTLINE OF THE STUDY

The credit effect can be viewed as a theory about the disposition of the revenue from money creation. In this theory the money created through credit expansion adds in the first instance to the supply of loanable funds. That is to say, new money adds to the demand for financial

[6] Another effect of anticipated price changes is on the demand for money balances. The public will hold smaller real balances when it expects prices to rise, and in consequence may accumulate more capital goods over time at the expense of real balances as a form of holding wealth.

The resulting increase in the capital-labor ratio of the economy can reduce the marginal productivity of capital and make the real rate of interest permanently lower than it would otherwise be. Such a shift in the relative stocks of real money balances and capital goods plays a role in monetary models of economic growth. It is ignored in this study.

assets, and in particular to the demand for those assets purchased through the expansion of credit. This raises two questions which are critically examined in Chapter 2. Does money creation in fact provide a revenue to the issuers—that is, to banks primarily—and, if so, do they save it? That they are supposed to save at least part of it is implied by the proposition that credit expansion adds to the supply of real loanable funds and thus reduces interest rates.

In Chapter 2, also, the services provided by banks in competing for deposits and the costs of these services are considered. These are often ignored in discussions pertaining to the costs of providing, and the returns to holding, deposit balances.

Chapters 3 through 5 are empirical analyses of short-run monetary effects on interest rates and include a test of the relative importance of the credit and portfolio effects. (Since the Fisher effect appears to have a long lag in periods of mild inflation, at least before 1966, the latest year covered here, it is ignored in this short-run analysis.) Both the credit and portfolio theories imply an inverse effect of the rate of change of the money stock on the level of interest rates. The evidence presented in Chapter 3 demonstrates this kind of inverse association.[7] The direction of influence can only be interpreted as running from monetary growth to interest rates, in support of the portfolio and credit theories. The evidence for the periods covered is not consistent with the reverse effect of interest rates on the money supply.

In Chapter 4 the credit theory is tested by extending the statistical analysis of Chapter 3. The test is based on a two-way division of monetary growth. Those sources of monetary growth due to credit expansion are one component and all other sources of growth are a residual component. The credit theory implies that the first source has much stronger effects on interest rates than the residual sources do and in effect ignores those other sources. Examples of other sources are federal expenditures financed by issuing new currency or reducing Treasury deposits at Federal Reserve banks, and foreign trade imbalances covered by transfers of gold or foreign exchange reserves. In

---

[7] Money is defined here as currency outside banks plus demand and time deposits of commercial banks, thus including all monetary liabilities of commercial banks.

testing the credit theory, the banking system should be consolidated with the Federal Reserve and the Treasury, although governmental agencies and commercial banks can be treated as different sources. The separation of the sources of monetary growth into those due to credit expansion and those due to residual components permits us to test whether their effects on interest rates differ.

In Chapter 5 the sources are examined in further detail: Bank credit is divided into loans and investments, to see whether they have differential effects on particular interest rates.

The statistical analysis indicates that, no matter how money is created, it affects interest rates inversely in the short run. The implication is that the first-round effect of money creation through credit expansion is weak, and that most of the effect on interest rates comes in subsequent rounds through the public's portfolio adjustments to the increase in monetary growth.

In Chapter 6 a simple mathematical model based on the portfolio effect described above is developed to account for this process. A change in monetary growth is assumed to produce a discrepancy between actual and desired money balances. The model describes how the subsequent adjustments temporarily affect interest rates.

The theory of the portfolio effect developed here implies a sequence of monetary effects on interest rates. To describe the sequence it is assumed that monetary growth increases and remains at a higher constant rate. Interest rates first decline and then gradually rise toward their initial position. Later, when the Fisher effect begins to take hold, nominal interest rates rise further. They go above the initial position, eventually by the amount of the increase in the rate of anticipated inflation. Apart from the Fisher effect, the movement to a new equilibrium need not be smooth but may, instead, involve overshooting and damped fluctuations around the long-run level.

Chapter 7 presents some estimates of this sequence. The inverse movement in interest rates, in response to a change in monetary growth, appears to reach its full effect in one to two quarters or so. After that, the movement changes direction. Interest rates pass their original position in three to five quarters. This evidence supports the portfolio theory. Monetary growth first affects interest rates inversely, but, because the portfolio effect is temporary and the credit effect weak, interest rates turn around, and eventually the Fisher effect carries them past their original level.

The results of this study are pertinent to various issues in monetary theory and policy which deal with the channels of monetary effects. One example is the alleged increase in aggregate expenditures which occurs when banks sell government securities in order to expand loans, a question widely discussed in the early 1950's. Another example is the "bills only" controversy of the early 1960's, in which the question was whether Federal Reserve open-market operations should be conducted in Treasury bills or bonds. The present results indicate that monetary effects do not depend greatly upon the means by which such operations are carried out. Whatever initial effects are produced in certain sectors of the money market are a small part of the total effect. That is not to say that all sectors of the economy respond the same way to monetary policy. But the response is not closely related to differences in the initial direction of issuing new money. The final chapter elaborates these implications of the results.

2

The Revenue from Money Creation and Its Disposition — a Theoretical Analysis

This chapter analyzes the effect of money creation on credit flows and interest rates. For present purposes several methods of money creation need to be treated separately. Currency issued by the government or a private group is one. Another is deposit expansion; franchises to supply deposit services may be granted by the government to a monopoly bank or, in a competitive system, to many banks.

The analysis takes up, first, the return obtained by issuers of money and, secondly, the manner in which they dispose of it. More specifically, we ask whether issuers of money obtain a net profit and, if so, whether such income is largely saved. If the income is saved, the total supply of real loanable funds will increase as a result of money creation; if it is spent for consumption, the total supply will be unchanged. The revenue, saving, and lending discussed here are to be understood as pertaining to *real* flows. Money creation will always increase these variables in nominal terms but will increase them in real terms only under special conditions.

The discussion is simplified by supposing that prices adjust immediately to monetary growth, that resources remain fully employed, and that any redistributions of wealth between debtors and creditors arising from unanticipated price changes can be disregarded. The discussion therefore pertains to positions of a moving equilibrium in which price changes are fully anticipated and short-run disturbances due to incomplete adjustments are ignored. Such an equilibrium will be most closely approximated when the rate of monetary growth is constant. We shall also consider later the implications of varying rates of monetary growth.

THE REVENUE FROM MONEY CREATION

Currency Issues

Suppose that the government or a franchised group of individuals prints and issues currency which need never be redeemed. For simplicity let this currency be the only money in existence and let the cost of issue and maintenance be negligible. (The irredeemability is critical, for a currency that can be exchanged on demand for some other money must have reserves behind it, and the operation is then equivalent to fractional reserve banking, discussed later.) There are three questions to be answered. At what rate will the currency be issued? What return do the issuers obtain, and what do they do with it? The answers to these questions will indicate the effect, if any, on interest rates. We start with the first two questions, leaving the third until the second part of the chapter.

The Optimal Rate of Issue. Printing and spending irredeemable currency provides disposable income to the issuers. If the new issues are fully anticipated by the public and prices rise commensurately, a higher rate of issue may increase or decrease the real income to the issuers, depending upon the elasticity of the public's demand for real money balances with respect to the rate of change of prices. Issuing money produces a tax on money holdings, in which the tax revenue is obtained by depreciation in the real value of outstanding holdings because of rising prices.[1] The outstanding holdings, the base of the tax, will diminish for higher rates of tax (that is, higher rates of price change), and the revenue depends upon the product of the base and the rate. Let M be the money stock; P, the price level; and t, time. The preceding revenue proposition is demonstrated by identity (3) derived as follows:

[1] M. Friedman, "Discussion of the Inflationary Gap," *Essays in Positive Economics,* Chicago, University of Chicago Press, 1963, pp. 251–62.

$$M \equiv (M/P)P \tag{1}$$

$$\frac{dM}{dt} \equiv \frac{M}{P}\frac{dP}{dt} + P\frac{d(M/P)}{dt} \tag{2}$$

$$\frac{dM}{Pdt} \equiv \frac{M}{P}\frac{dP}{Pdt} + \frac{d(M/P)}{dt} \tag{3}$$

where dM/Pdt is the revenue per period of time in real terms. M/P is determined by the demand for money balances and, among other variables, depends upon real income, X, and the rate of price change, dP/Pdt. If real money balances are unchanging, we have, dropping the last term of (3),

$$\frac{dM}{Pdt} = \frac{M}{P}\frac{dP}{Pdt}. \tag{4}$$

M/P is the base to which the tax on money balances applies, and dP/Pdt is the tax rate.

If X is growing, desired M/P will also expand over time, and this allows growth of the money stock at the same rate without a rise in prices. We may assume with no important loss of generality that M/P is proportional to X (that is, that the income elasticity of real money balances is unity). Then we have, similar to (3),

$$\frac{dM}{PXdt} \equiv \frac{M}{PX}\left(\frac{dX}{Xdt} + \frac{dP}{Pdt}\right) + \frac{d(M/PX)}{dt} \tag{5}$$

where M/PX depends on dP/Pdt. For a constant rate of price change, M/PX will have a corresponding constant equilibrium value. In the long run this value will be attained and remain constant if the rate of price change is constant.[2] If real money balances are unchanging, we have, similar to (4),

$$\frac{dM}{PXdt} = \frac{M}{PX}\left(\frac{dX}{Xdt} + \frac{dP}{Pdt}\right). \tag{6}$$

This equation expresses the revenue obtained from issuing money as a

[2] Other variables which affect the demand for money, such as interest rates, are ignored for the moment. For an analysis of the case in which the income elasticity is not unity, see M. Friedman, "Government Revenue from Inflation," *Journal of Political Economy*, July/August 1971, pp. 846–56.

ratio to national income. The revenue comprises two parts, one obtained by supplying the desired growth in balances due to rising real income, and an additional part obtained by increasing prices.

Note the situation when the money stock is constant and

$$-dX/Xdt = dP/Pdt. \qquad (6a)$$

Here prices decline at the rate of growth of real income. The continual appreciation in the real value of money provides an income (not counted by conventional accounting practices) to individual holders which they collectively "use" to accumulate real balances in order to keep constant the desired ratio of money to national income. The power to create money allows the issuers to collect this revenue, which they can do by issuing money at the rate $dM/Mdt = dX/Xdt$.

Among different rates of issue and corresponding rates of price change, the revenue, N, expressed as a percentage of national income, has a maximum value. It is found by differentiating with respect to the rate of price change. Let $dP/Pdt = \pi$ and $dX/Xdt = g$ (a given growth rate independent of π). Then, from (6),

$$N = (M/PX)(g + \pi), \qquad (6b)$$

and

$$\frac{\partial N}{\partial \pi} = \frac{\partial (M/PX)}{\partial \pi}(g + \pi) + \frac{M}{PX} = 0. \qquad (7)$$

This equation can be simplified by making use of the expression for the elasticity of demand for real balances with respect to the rate of price change (assumed to be correctly anticipated). Usually this elasticity is defined as

$$\frac{\partial (M/PX)}{\partial \pi} \frac{\pi}{M/PX},$$

which has a sign opposite to that of π because $\partial (M/PX)/\partial \pi$ is always negative. However, it is better to define the elasticity in the present context as [3]

---

[3] I am indebted to Alvin Marty for this point and other suggestions for improving this chapter.

$$\xi \equiv \frac{\partial(M/PX)}{\partial(\pi + g)} \frac{\pi + g}{M/PX}$$

or, assuming g is constant,

$$\xi = \frac{\partial(M/PX)}{\partial\pi} \frac{\pi + g}{M/PX} \tag{8}$$

where the ordinate of the demand curve for money balances is expressed in terms of $\pi + g$. The justification is that the revenue from money creation is positive so long as $\pi + g$ is positive, irrespective of the sign of π alone. If in this way we define ξ to be negative when the revenue is positive, the expression for finding the maximum revenue is simplified. Substituting (8) into (7) we obtain

$$\partial N/\partial\pi = \xi + 1 = 0. \tag{9}$$

Revenue is maximized when ξ, the elasticity of demand with respect to the rate of change of nominal income, equals -1. This is the standard monopoly solution. Marginal revenue is zero at that point, as is also marginal cost, since costs of issue are assumed to be negligible.[4]

By what device do money holders actually "pay" the tax revenue shown by (6b), that is, how do they transfer real resources to the issuers of new money? The holders continually use part of their income to keep their depreciating nominal balances at the desired real level. Hence their expenditures are lower by that amount, and the goods and services thus given up are purchased by the issuers of new money.

A Specified Rate of Issue.   The previous analysis assumes that the issuer of money is free to choose the rate of issue. Suppose, however, that the rate is determined by market conditions. The issuer must then

---

[4] This result is well known and was presented in my study "The Monetary Dynamics of Hyperinflation," in M. Friedman (ed.), *Studies in the Quantity Theory of Money,* Chicago, University of Chicago Press, 1956.

There is a problem, should adjustments be instantaneous. If the demand for money were to adjust immediately to the current rate of price change, inflation would be self-generating. For the solution given in the text, it must be assumed that demand adjusts with a sufficient lag to produce a stable equilibrium. With a lagged adjustment, however, the revenue can be increased indefinitely by increasing the rate of issue, which produces accelerating inflation. Therefore, if the revenue is to remain constant over the long run, the rate of issue must be constant. See *ibid.*

take the rate as given. If the rate increases, the effect on the revenue in the long run depends upon the elasticity of the demand curve. If the demand is elastic ($\xi < -1$), the revenue declines; if inelastic, the revenue increases.

The available evidence suggests that the demand is inelastic for moderate to high rates of price change. For seven hyperinflations, I estimated that the maximum constant revenue was reached with rates over 100 per cent per year.[5] Other studies have obtained similar results[6] and also suggest that the demand is inelastic for low rates of price change. So long as the public is on an inelastic part of its demand curve, an increase in the monetary growth rate produces a larger revenue.

A given rate is relevant to banks, which maintain a reserve ratio and therefore are dependent on the growth of their reserves to expand. There are other complications for banks, too, since the assumption of zero cost is not appropriate for deposits, even as a first approximation.

Deposit Expansion of a Monopoly Bank

With banking, the total money stock consists of currency and bank deposits held by the public. (Whether time deposits are included or not makes no difference for present analytical purposes.) Since currency and deposits can be exchanged on demand, a monopoly bank will maintain some ratio of required and excess reserves to deposits in the long run. Reserves comprise non-interest-bearing currency and central-bank monetary liabilities — that is, high-powered money. The profits of the bank per period of time are the interest from earning assets held over the period, E, less the cost of interest or services on deposits, T, plus any increase in its assets from deposit expansion over the period. For the first item we have

$$E \equiv (1 - r)Di \tag{10}$$

[5] *Ibid.*

[6] See Maurice Allais, "A Restatement of the Quantity Theory of Money," *American Economic Review,* December 1966, pp. 1123–56. See also studies by Colin Campbell, John Deaver, and Adolfo Diz, in David Meiselman (ed.), *Varieties of Monetary Experience,* Chicago, University of Chicago Press, 1970; and Teh-wei Hu, "Hyperinflation and the Dynamics of the Demand for Money in China, 1945–49," *Journal of Political Economy,* January/February 1971, pp. 186–95.

where i is the nominal rate of interest net of lending costs on earning assets and $(1 - r)$ is the ratio of earning assets to deposits, D. If r is 10 per cent, each deposit created by the bank is accompanied by an increase in reserves of one-tenth and in earning assets of nine-tenths.

When prices are rising, we may calculate the real earnings on the initial stock of assets, E/P, allowing for the depreciation in the real value of the principal. Two adjustments are needed. First, we must convert the dollar amount of earnings in (10) to real terms by deflating by an appropriate price index. Second, since the *initial* stock of assets (including reserves) depreciates in real terms by $(D/P)\pi$, where π as before is the rate of rise in prices, this amount of depreciation must be deducted from earnings to give the real rate of return. These adjustments give

$$[(1 - r)Di - D\pi]/P. \tag{11}$$

Except for the conversion to real terms, (11) treats gross earnings according to conventional accounting practice.

The second item noted above as affecting bank profits is interest and service costs on deposits. Total costs depend on the rate of interest paid and services provided per deposit dollar and on the total quantity of real deposits. (For given real deposits, the costs of expanding nominal deposits are assumed negligible.) Service costs are introduced into the analysis later.

The third component of bank profits, increases in assets per period of time, is an unconventional item not included in published statements of earnings. Bank accountants treat an expansion of deposits as adding equally to both assets and liabilities; but if the earnings added for each new deposit exceed the costs, the present value of future income streams — that is, net worth — will increase. Continual increases in net worth due to deposit expansion may be viewed for our purposes as *current* income. Whether this income would in fact be used to increase net worth rather than be paid to stockholders or depositors will be considered later. (Some of it might be used to make up for the depreciation in real value of assets, which was deducted from earnings in equation 11.) How the income is used makes no difference here; it is simply the flow of income to the bank from the expansion of nominal deposits. The increase in total assets from deposit expansion is dD/dt, or in real terms, dD/Pdt.

This can be expressed in a more convenient form. For a given reserve ratio and fraction of money balances held as currency outside banks, C, deposits and total money balances grow at the same rate. That is, $M \equiv C + D$ and $D \equiv [1 - (C/M)]M$; if C/M is constant, $dD/Ddt = dM/Mdt$. We shall ignore growth in real income and assume that real money balances desired by the public have a zero growth rate. This simplification makes no substantive difference. Then the price level and deposits grow at related rates. That is, $M \equiv (M/P)P$ and, if M/P is constant, $dM/Mdt = dP/Pdt$ and, from above, we have $dD/Ddt = dP/Pdt$ or

$$dD/Pdt = (D/P)(dP/Pdt) \equiv (D/P)\,\pi. \qquad (12)$$

This expresses the real revenue of the bank from deposit expansion as proportional to real deposits times the rate of change of prices.

We can define net profits per period of time, N, measured in dollars of constant purchasing power, as the sum of (11) and (12) minus total costs in real terms, T.

$$N = (1 - r)(D/P)i - (D/P)\,\pi + (D/P)\,\pi - T$$
$$= (1 - r)(D/P)i - T. \qquad (13)$$

The first part of (13) shows that the gross *real* income of a bank equals its earning assets *measured in real terms* times the *nominal* rate of interest.[7]

The revenue from expansion makes up for the continual depreciation in the real value of the bank's financial assets. The nominal rate of interest is assumed to be exogenous to the bank, at least for the long-run equilibrium analyzed here. The rate of price change, π, is ultimately determined by the expansion of high-powered money (if r, C/M, and M/P remain constant). D/P is variable; it depends upon the opportunity cost to the public of holding deposits (i if the alternative is financial assets, and π if the alternative is real capital or goods) and

---

[7] The nominal rate of interest, i, in (13) may be viewed as composed of the real rate of interest plus π. Banks earn a real return on their deposits equal to the real rate of interest plus the rate of inflation, the latter reflecting the revenue from deposit expansion. It is assumed here that $di/d\pi = 1$, that is, the real rate of interest is given.

the quantity and quality of services and interest which the bank chooses to provide on deposits.

The Optimal Services on Deposits. Banks have always provided the service of clearing checks and bookkeeping for depositors' accounts. Banks also used to pay interest on some demand deposits, but interest payments on such deposits have been prohibited since 1933. In the years since then banks have expanded services on checking accounts and have adopted various devices that amount to the indirect payment of interest (such as charging less for loans if the borrower keeps compensating balances with the bank). Even in those communities where banks have succeeded in establishing and maintaining a tight cartel to obtain monopoly profits, they would not for that reason provide no services at all. On large accounts today, banks offer a variety of bookkeeping services and lines of credit. On small accounts for individuals, one important and costly service is the regular provision of currency, requiring numerous branch offices at convenient locations. Credit cards have far to go to make currency obsolete.

Nonbranch banking laws and other statutory regulations constitute an important barrier to the competitive provision of services on small accounts. Any employed person who does his shopping after work or on weekends must wonder about the still restricted business hours of most of our banks, which perpetuate an earlier tradition of offering to sell currency as infrequently as possible. Although there are some restrictions on the expansion of worthwhile services for nonbusiness accounts, there appears to be room for expanded and improved services if earnings justify them. The cost of servicing deposits is generally ignored in theories of the banking system on the grounds that they are constant.[8] This is highly dubious for demand deposits, particularly because the prohibition of interest payments induces banks to compete through services.

---

[8] Two recent articles which recognize in different ways the importance of servicing costs are John H. Karekin, "Commercial Banks and the Supply of Money: A Market-Determined Demand Deposit Rate," *Federal Reserve Bulletin,* October 1967, pp. 1699–1712; and Don Patinkin, "Money and Wealth: A Review Article," *Journal of Economic Literature,* December 1969, pp. 1140–60, especially pp. 1150–51. See also Benjamin Klein, "The Payment of Interest on Commercial Bank Deposits and the Price of Money: A Study of the Demand for Money," Ph.D. dissertation, University of Chicago, 1970.

FIGURE 2-1

Marginal and Average Cost of Deposit Services

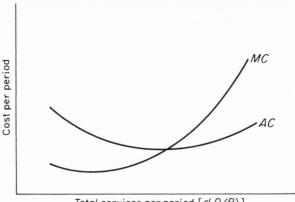

Total services per period $[s(D/P)]$

To take account of bank services, we may view them as a flow per period of time like any other business or consumer service. Let us assume that the service flow can be assigned a dollar value which measures for depositors the quality and amount of service. Then we can express the service flow per period of time as a percentage of the average deposit dollar; call this percentage per year s, a nonpecuniary rate of return like the pecuniary interest rate. Note that s measures the rate of return to depositors, not the cost of providing the services. Defining and measuring the value to consumers of improvements in quality entail some problems, which we shall disregard.

The total quantity of services supplied in real terms is $s(D/P)$. By varying s, a bank can affect the quantity of real deposits demanded of it. The relation of the cost to the quantity supplied can be represented by cost curves like those for any product and presumably are subject to the standard economies and diseconomies of scale.[9] They are illustrated in Figure 2-1. (If s takes the form solely of interest payments,

---

[9] The value of s will depend in part upon the amount of excess reserves held, since this affects the liquidity of the bank and its ability to convert deposits into currency on demand. This dependence can be ignored here, since r is assumed not to change.

The total real cost of providing a given flow of services on deposits is assumed to depend on the real value of deposits and not to vary with changes in the nominal quantity of deposits.

there are constant costs to scale and $dT/d(D/P) = s$, a special case discussed later.) It is conceivable that the costs of providing more services may be different depending upon whether s or D/P rises; such complications are ignored here.[10]

The level of services provided is set by a monopoly bank to maximize net profits, N. For a given π and i the maximum [11] N is found by partial differentiation of (13) with respect to s. The differentiation gives (Q denotes sD/P)

$$\frac{\partial N}{\partial s} = (1 - r)i\,\frac{\partial(D/P)}{\partial s} - \left[\frac{D}{P} + s\,\frac{\partial(D/P)}{\partial s}\right]\frac{dT}{dQ} = 0$$
$$= \qquad MR_s \qquad - \qquad MC_s \qquad = 0$$

(14)

where MR and MC represent the marginal revenue and marginal cost of services. Equation 14 may be interpreted as setting marginal revenue equal to marginal cost according to the traditional formulation of profit maximization.

The variable which the bank controls to maximize profits is not the total quantity of real deposits or of services supplied, however, but the services provided per deposit dollar. (The total cost, of course, still depends upon the flow of total services supplied.) The bank increases services until the additional revenue just matches the increase in cost.

---

[10] Growth in real income produces growth in desired and actual real deposits. This affects the discounted value of the future growth in costs. Since growth in real income is assumed to occur independently of any expansion by banks of nominal deposits, we may ignore changes in real deposits and costs associated with growth in real income. However, a profit-maximizing bank would take account of the potential growth in real deposits and therefore in future profits due to income growth. A more complete analysis should allow for this.

[11] Letting $Q = sD/P$, the second derivative becomes, after eliminating s by applying (14),

$$\frac{\partial^2 N}{\partial s^2} = \frac{d^2 T}{dQ^2}\left[\frac{(1 - r)i\,\dfrac{\partial(D/P)}{\partial s}}{\dfrac{dT}{dQ}}\right]^2 - \frac{dT}{dQ}\left[2\,\frac{\partial(D/P)}{\partial s} - \frac{\dfrac{D}{P}\,\dfrac{\partial^2(D/P)}{\partial s^2}}{\dfrac{\partial(D/P)}{\partial s}}\right].$$

This will be negative, indicating that (14) specifies a maximum point, under the sufficient conditions that dT/dQ and d^2T/dQ^2 are positive (which means that marginal cost is positive and rising, respectively), and that $\partial(D/P)/\partial s$ and $\partial^2(D/P)/\partial s^2$ are positive and negative, respectively (which means that the marginal effect of s on the demand for real deposits is positive but diminishing).

Given the quality provided, the total quantity of services supplied, $s(D/P)$, depends upon the demand. Consequently, while the bank determines nominal deposits, it does not directly control their real value, which is determined by the public in the light of s, i, and π. The profit maximization is illustrated in Figure 2-2. The two terms of equation 14 are graphed in the top part of the figure, with s on the horizontal axis. The demand for real deposits (for given i and π) is represented in the bottom part. It has been conventionally drawn to increase by diminishing amounts as s increases. With such a demand curve, the marginal revenue term of (14) declines as s increases, and the marginal cost term rises. At the intersection, the corresponding values of s and D/P

FIGURE 2-2

Value of s That Maximizes Net Profits

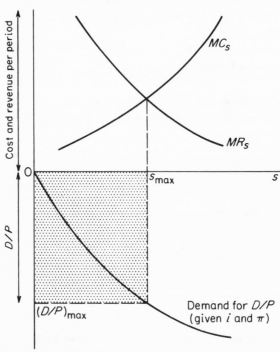

Shaded area = $s(D/P)$ which maximizes net profits.

FIGURE 2-3

Average Cost and Maximum Profits [a]

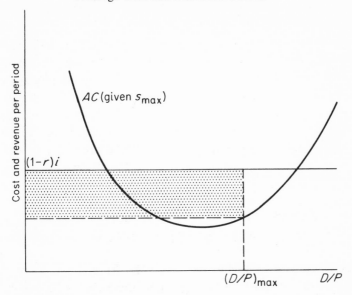

Shaded area = N_{max}.

[a] Given s_{max} and $(D/P)_{max}$ from Figure 2-2.

determine the total services supplied, shown by the shaded area. These values are used in Figure 2-3 to find the average cost and net profit per deposit dollar and the maximum total profits (shaded area). (Note that, if π changes, the maximizing value of s changes, thereby shifting the AC curve in Figure 2-3.)

Interest Payments on Deposits. Despite its prohibition, the payment of interest raises interesting and relevant theoretical points for this discussion.

If s is the rate of interest paid on deposits, total cost in real terms is simply $T = s(D/P)$. Average and marginal cost are assumed to be constant and equal to the given value of s. The net profit to the bank may be derived by writing (13) as follows:

$$N = (D/P)[(1 - r)i - s] \tag{15}$$

with a maximum given by

$$\frac{\partial N}{\partial s} = [(1 - r)i - s]\frac{\partial(D/P)}{\partial s} - \frac{D}{P} = 0. \tag{16}$$

Interest payments offset the cost to the public of holding deposits, which for present purposes may be represented by the rate of interest foregone if the deposit is not invested in an interest-bearing asset. The demand for deposit balances depends upon the difference in the rate of return on deposits, s, and on other assets, i (assumed the same as for the bank). The value of the demand elasticity with respect to $i - s$ which maximizes profits according to (16) is (i constant)

$$\frac{\partial(D/P)}{\partial(-s)}\frac{(i - s)}{D/P} = \frac{-1}{1 - [ri/(i - s)]}. \tag{17}$$

In the special case of no reserves ($r = 0$), the left-hand side of equation 17 reduces to -1, which reformulates the previous proposition about maximum profits to state that a monopoly bank which holds no reserves will provide services up to the point where the elasticity of demand for real deposits with respect to the public's cost of holding them is minus unity. The bank thus maximizes its profits by keeping the public's cost constant. Therefore, an exogenous change in the rate of inflation does not affect the public's cost or the bank's profits.

If r is not zero, the bank's profit in providing deposits is less than the public's cost of holding them. The consequences can be seen from (17), which has a greater negative value than minus unity. Instead of operating where the demand elasticity is -1, the bank operates at a more elastic part of the demand curve.

The Effect of Changes in Monetary Growth on Profits.   What happens to profits when the rate of growth of money and prices is increased? To find the answer we may derive $dN/d\pi$ subject to the condition that $\partial N/\partial s = 0$. From (13) we obtain, assuming $di/d\pi = 1$ (see note 7, above),

$$\frac{dN}{d\pi} = (1 - r)\left[\frac{D}{P} + i\,\frac{\partial(D/P)}{\partial\pi} + i\,\frac{\partial(D/P)}{\partial s}\frac{ds}{d\pi}\right]$$

$$- \frac{dT}{dQ}\left[\frac{D}{P}\frac{ds}{d\pi} + s\,\frac{\partial(D/P)}{\partial\pi} + s\,\frac{\partial(D/P)}{\partial s}\frac{ds}{d\pi}\right]. \tag{18}$$

Rearranging terms we have

$$\frac{dN}{d\pi} = (1 - r)\left[\frac{D}{P} + i\,\frac{\partial(D/P)}{\partial\pi}\right] - \frac{dT}{dQ}\,s\,\frac{\partial(D/P)}{\partial\pi}$$

$$+ \frac{ds}{d\pi}\left\{(1 - r)i\,\frac{\partial(D/P)}{\partial s} - \frac{dT}{dQ}\left[\frac{D}{P} + s\,\frac{\partial(D/P)}{\partial s}\right]\right\}. \quad (19)$$

The differential $ds/d\pi$ shows the adjustment of s by banks to changes in π to maintain the maximum level of profits. By (14) this condition requires the second line to be zero. The expression can therefore be written

$$\frac{dN}{d\pi} = (1 - r)\frac{D}{P}\,(1 + \xi_i) - \frac{dT}{dQ}\,s\,\frac{\partial(D/P)}{\partial\pi} \quad (20)$$

for $\partial N/\partial s = 0$ and where ξ_i is the elasticity of demand for real money balances with respect to i. The second part is definitely positive, since the partial derivative there is negative. Unless the demand to hold deposits is elastic (that is, a greater negative number than minus unity), the first term will also be positive, and profits will increase with a rise in π. The demand must be highly elastic to render (20) negative.

An intuitive explanation of this result is that an increase in π lowers D/P, which tends to reduce costs. If ξ_i is inelastic, revenues rise. Hence net profits increase. Also, as a result of an increase in π, s may increase or decrease, but this does not affect the result. Condition 14 — that $\partial N/\partial s = 0$ — specifies that any small change in s will not affect profits.

Deposit Expansion of a Banking System

Determination of Aggregate Real Deposits. If many banks are in competition, an individual bank takes the flow of services provided by other banks as given and either provides an equivalent flow or goes out of business.[12] The individual bank, like any firm in a competitive market, can vary the quantity of deposits supplied — in this case both in real as well as in nominal terms. This differs from a monopoly bank,

---

[12] Monopolistic competition could be analyzed by making the appropriate assumptions. That case will not be treated here except to consider below the existing situation in which there is competition among banks but lack of free entry.

which directly controls only the nominal quantity of deposits supplied. Total real deposits are determined, through price level changes, by the public's desired real balances. A monopoly bank can affect desired real deposits only by making changes in s. Contrariwise, an individual bank in a truly competitive system takes s as given, and changes in the supply of nominal deposits by one bank do not perceptibly affect prices. Consequently, from the individual bank's point of view, it supplies real deposit balances (that is, P is taken as given). The position of maximum profit is therefore found by differentiating (13) with respect to D/P for a given s:

$$\frac{\partial N}{\partial (D/P)} = (1 - r)i - s\frac{dT}{dQ} = 0$$
$$= MR - MC = 0,$$

(21)

which may be interpreted as requiring that the increase in revenue and the increase in cost of adding one more dollar of deposits be equal (s, r, i, and P are taken as given to the bank by the market). The relevant curves for an individual bank are illustrated in Figure 2-4. The bank will operate at the point where the two marginal curves intersect.

The sum of real deposits supplied by all banks at each level of s describes an aggregate supply curve for the system, illustrated in Figure 2-5. Equilibrium is attained through changes in s by banks

FIGURE 2-4

Marginal Revenue and Cost for One Bank in a System

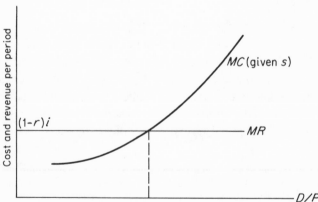

FIGURE 2-5

Aggregate Demand and Supply for Real Deposits

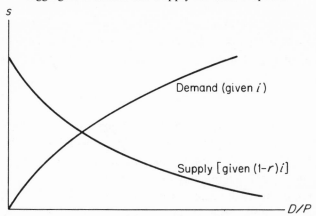

acting individually to supply the quantity of deposits which maximizes their profits. For example, an increase in s attracts more real deposits to a bank (and, for a general increase in s, more to all banks in the aggregate through an inflow of currency reserves and, ceteris paribus, fall in the price level as the public demands larger real money balances). At the same time an increase in s raises the marginal cost curve in Figure 2-4 and reduces the quantity of real deposits which maximizes bank profits. Adjustments by all banks continue until an equilibrium for the system is attained as depicted by the intersection of the curves in Figure 2-5; this position (given r and i) is consistent with profit maximization by each bank.

If the banking system lacks free entry, net profits can be positive. This reflects a net return to the banking franchise. In terms of Figure 2-4 it means that banks operate at a point to the right of the minimum average cost so that average revenue exceeds average cost.[13]

---

[13] If we substitute (21) into (13), we have $N = (D/P)s(dT/dQ) - T$. Dividing by $s(D/P)$ we obtain net profit per unit of service provided:

$$N/Q = (dT/dQ) - AC,$$

that is, marginal cost minus average cost, which can remain positive only in the absence of free entry. A positive value means that measured costs exclude the imputed value of the banking franchise.

The Effect of Changes in Monetary Growth on Profits. With a change in monetary growth and thus in the rate of price change, the effect on profits may be found, from (18), under the conditions of profit maximization for a competitive system given by (21). Equation 18 was derived without regard to the number of banks and so pertains to any banking system. Substituting the competitive solution of (21) into (18) gives

$$dN/d\pi = (D/P)\left[(1 - r) - (dT/dQ)(ds/d\pi)\right]. \tag{22}$$

Whether profits rise, fall, or remain unchanged with an increase in the rate of monetary growth and of price change depends upon the relative size of these terms. No general conclusion can be established.

The sign of (22) is ambiguous partly because $ds/d\pi$ is always positive (making the two terms within the brackets of opposite sign), since a higher rate of price change raises both curves in Figure 2-5 and thus definitely raises s. The demand curve shifts to the left for an increase in π, because people now want smaller real deposit balances for the same level of services. The supply curve in Figure 2-5 shifts to the right, because a higher π increases the profit on each deposit dollar, and banks want to supply more real deposits. The intersection therefore occurs at a higher level of s, but at more, less, or the same quantity of real deposits, depending upon the relative amount of the shifts in the two curves.[14]

That $ds/d\pi$ is positive can also be demonstrated by differentiating implicity the right-hand side of equation (21) with respect to π.

$$\frac{ds}{d\pi} = \frac{(1 - r) - s^2 \dfrac{d^2T}{dQ^2} \dfrac{\partial(D/P)}{\partial \pi}}{\dfrac{dT}{dQ} + s \dfrac{d^2T}{dQ^2}\left(s \dfrac{\partial(D/P)}{\partial s} + \dfrac{D}{P}\right)}. \tag{23}$$

All these factors are positive except $\partial(D/P)/\partial\pi$, which is negative, so that all terms and the entire expression are positive. Since $ds/d\pi$ is positive, we cannot establish the sign of (22) and thereby determine the effect of monetary growth on profits without further information.

---

[14] As pointed out above, this result is not true for a monopoly bank. It supplies the rate of services which maximizes its profits. This could involve a decrease in services when π rises.

To see what additional information is required, we may derive the condition for a positive effect of π on N. According to (22) this condition requires

$$ds/d\pi < \frac{1-r}{dT/dQ}. \tag{24}$$

This will be satisfied, according to (23), if

$$\frac{-s\,\dfrac{\partial(D/P)}{\partial\pi}}{s\,\dfrac{\partial(D/P)}{\partial s}+\dfrac{D}{P}} < \frac{1-r}{dT/dQ}, \tag{25}$$

assuming d^2T/dQ^2 is not zero (discussed later). Further simplification occurs if we introduce expressions for the two elasticities of demand, namely

$$\xi_i = \frac{\partial(D/P)}{\partial\pi}\,\frac{i}{D/P},$$

the same as in equation 20, which assumes $di/d\pi = 1$, and

$$\xi_s = \frac{\partial(D/P)}{\partial s}\,\frac{s}{D/P}.$$

We may also make use of (21), the condition for profit maximization. Substituting into (25), we have, after simplification,

$$-\xi_i < 1 + \xi_s, \tag{26}$$

that is, profits increase when the rate of inflation goes up, so long as the (absolute value of the) elasticity of demand with respect to the interest rate is less than unity plus the elasticity with respect to services. If the interest elasticity of demand is inelastic (that is, less than unity in absolute value), profits will necessarily increase, because the services elasticity would never be less than zero. Profits will still increase even if the interest elasticity exceeds unity in absolute value, so long as the services elasticity exceeds zero by a greater amount. Actually, it seems most likely that the absolute value of these two elasticities would be about the same, which would insure that (26) holds.

The intuitive explanation for this result lies in the increase in revenue per deposit dollar caused by an increase in π. As a result banks are induced to increase services; while this raises costs, it also raises the demand for deposits and so also revenues. If the proportionate effect of higher π on the demand for deposits is not too large relative to the effect of an induced increase in s, revenues will increase and, except in the special cases discussed next, will not be offset by increases in costs, causing net profits to rise.

Free Entry and Interest Payments.   Profits will be exactly zero in the long run under two special conditions. If there is free entry, new banks will be established to take advantage of any attractions of the banking business. Competition for deposits will force banks to raise s and increase the costs of supplying services until economic profits are zero (allowing for the prevailing return on capital). Average cost for each bank will rise until its minimum point passes through the intersection of the MC and MR curves shown in Figure 2-4. Then $MR = AC$ in long-run equilibrium, and profits will be zero.

If s represents solely interest paid on deposits, total costs, as noted before, are $s(D/P)$, since there are no diseconomies of scale in the payment of interest. Hence $dT/d[s(D/P)] = 1$ and (21) implies that $s = (1 - r)i$. Substituting into (15) shows that profits are then zero. Competition among existing banks forces them to pay any and all returns from money creation to depositors. Obviously, in this case, deposit expansion does not change bank profits or net worth in real terms. In the absence of interest payments average cost curves rise in terms of the services provided, and it is possible in equilibrium for marginal cost to exceed average cost. When this occurs, banks receive net profits in real terms.

Conclusion.   The preceding analysis shows that a higher average rate of monetary growth is most likely to raise bank profits in real terms. That result depends upon the assumption that demand for real deposits is either inelastic to changes in the rate of price change or not greater in absolute value than unity plus the demand elasticity with respect to services on deposits. The result also assumes that in the United States today there is competition among banks but restricted entry, and that banks are free to recover all of the revenue from money creation by charging for loans what the market will bear. Given a rise in bank profits from deposit expansion, the next question concerns how it is used.

DISPOSITION OF THE REVENUE:
THE EFFECT ON SAVING

What happens to the real revenue from money creation? A common answer to this question is that money creation adds in the first instance to investment expenditures, because the banking system creates most new money by a process of lending or purchasing assets. Of course, money creation expands deposits and bank assets in nominal terms. But this proposition asserts that money creation also increases bank lending in real terms because, as explained above, money creation imposes an inflation tax on money balances which provides a revenue in real terms to banks. With this addition to the supply of real loanable funds, equilibrium between total borrowing and lending occurs at a lower rate of interest, since the demand schedule for loanable funds is assumed to remain unchanged. This proposition was referred to in the first chapter as the credit effect on interest rates.

The process of bank credit expansion has been called "forced saving," [15] since the economy thus diverts more resources to capital formation than the nonbanking public had intended via individual decisions to abstain from consumption. Forced saving reflects an institutional characteristic of the monetary system, since in a free-exchange economy resources are otherwise allocated to reflect the preferences of individual consumers and lenders. By such a process the free-banking era in the United States in the first half of the 1800's supposedly helped to finance the industrial development of the West.

Once we ask how it can be that institutional arrangements "force" the economy to save more than it wants to, we recognize that there is nothing necessary about such an outcome at all. The institutions which create and dispose of new money have options on how to use it. To carry out public policy the government or its central bank may lend money to certain eligible borrowers. Why, however, should commercial banks use their power to create money to accumulate financial assets? Why not increase consumption instead? It is true that banks by their nature hold financial assets as the counterpart to deposit liabilities, but the owners of banks do not have to take the benefits of

[15] F. A. Hayek, "A Note on the Development of the Doctrine of 'Forced Saving,'" *Quarterly Journal of Economics,* November 1932, pp. 123–33.

money creation as a future income stream on financial assets: they can sell their rights to the stream and spend the capitalized sum immediately.

One may therefore raise questions about the proposition of forced saving. Further analysis will bring out the assumptions implicit in the proposition. It is desirable to discuss separately the various kinds of monetary expansion, namely, money creation by the government, by a group of individuals, and by banks (not distinguishing for present purposes between a monopoly and a banking system).

Government Currency Issues to Finance Deficits

Government expenditures affect the allocation of resources, whether financed by new money, issues of securities, or taxation. The net effect depends upon the extent to which government expenditures are comparable to and are taken into account in private spending. Some government expenditures may substitute for related private expenditures and so produce little effect on the allocation of total expenditures. Similarly, the use of tax revenues to retire government debt may not affect total saving. While this action adds to the potential supply of funds available for private lending, at the same time it reduces future government interest payments and so reduces the liability of taxpayers to provide the revenue for such payments. The present discounted value to taxpayers of the reduction in future taxes for bond interest equals the value of debt retired.[16] There is, therefore, no change in taxpayers' net worth, and the money received in exchange for the government bonds is equivalent to a remission of taxes. Such an increase in disposable income will not ordinarily affect the allocation of household expenditures between consumption and saving. There is no addition to loanable funds from the debt retirement other than what is normally produced by a shift in the disposition of income from the public to the private sector.

The same argument applies to the retirement of government bonds

---

[16] This requires that the discount factor applied to future taxes equal the interest rate on government debt. If the equality does not hold, redistributive effects occur. See B. Pesek and T. Saving, *Money, Wealth, and Economic Theory*, New York, Macmillan, 1967, Chap. 10. See also R. Mundell, "The Public Debt, Corporate Income Taxes, and the Rate of Interest," *Journal of Political Economy*, December 1960, pp. 622–26.

by issues of new money, which impose a tax on money balances via the accompanying rise in prices. To the extent that taxpayers act like "stockholders of the government," they will tend not to be influenced by an increase in the current tax on money balances, since it will be exactly offset by a reduction in the present value of future tax payments for bond interest. In practice, the foresight and willingness of taxpayers to behave as stockholders in this way may be less than perfect, and there may be redistributional effects among households, but the effect of government money creation on saving and on interest rates does not differ in principle from expenditures financed by other forms of taxation and depends in each instance upon the particular measures adopted. No general conclusions can be drawn about the direction or magnitude of the effects.

Private Currency Issues [17]

A franchise to supply currency (without obligation to redeem it) bestows an annual income equal to the value per year of the currency issued if the cost of printing and maintaining it in circulation is ignored. The issuers can spend the new money just as though they had first received it as income. If they treat this flow of purchasing power like other income, they will spend most of it on consumer goods and services and save the remainder by purchasing various kinds of assets. The division between saving and consumption need be no different than that for other sources of income. Furthermore, the ratio of saving to income in the economy at large need not change — and most likely would not greatly — provided that the saving habits of the issuers were typical of the economy as a whole. In that event, interest rates and the allocation of expenditures would not be affected.

If the franchise to issue currency is not permanent, the income stream no longer lasts forever, and the preceding conclusion must be qualified. Suppose that the amount of money issued under the franchise varies over time in an uncertain way or that the franchise has a limited life. Creating money then provides a variable or limited income stream, which affects saving because most people do not like their con-

---

[17] I am indebted to Milton Friedman for suggesting the following argument. John Scadding also makes some of the same points in his proposed University of Chicago Ph.D. dissertation.

sumption to vary with fluctuations in income. The issuers will seek to maintain a fairly even level of consumption at some fraction of the expected average income stream. For a limited-life franchise, the expected discounted value of the income stream is equivalent to some lower, permanent level of income. For a variable stream, people tend to maintain consumption when receipts fall temporarily below average. Real saving can thus be expected to increase for sudden, apparently temporary increases in the rate of money creation and to decline for temporary decreases in the rate. An uncertain income stream might also lead people to play it safe against unanticipated declines by saving more on the average.

For various reasons, therefore, a franchise to issue money may affect real saving in the economy, but not dollar for dollar of the amount issued. Saving resulting from money creation will depend instead upon deviations of monetary growth from its long-run expected rate, being in real terms higher when new issues exceed the expected rate and lower when new issues fall short. If money creation had the same variability as most other sources of income, the effect on real saving would on the average be zero. None of these effects on saving are "forced," but are the result of voluntary decisions of economic units made in response to an uncertain and variable income stream.

It is important to emphasize our assumption of no redistributional effects from inflation other than the tax on money balances. In the literature, "forced" saving is sometimes attributed to a lag of nominal wages behind prices, causing workers' real incomes to fall and business real income to rise. If workers have the smaller propensity to save out of income, the effect of this redistribution is to increase saving. Such effects are assumed away in the present analysis in order to focus on the credit effects.

Deposit Expansion by Banks

Since banks are obligated to meet requests for deposit withdrawals, newly created deposits are not used, in contrast to irredeemable currency, by the issuers directly for their personal disposition. Yet the institutional practices of banking make a difference more of form than of substance. When a bank expands deposits, it obtains a revenue the size of which in real terms depends upon the rate of expansion, the costs of operating the bank, the number of banks, and the restrictions on entry, as discussed above. To be sure, bankers would probably not regard the revenue as a tax on deposits. From their point of view, the expansion of assets merely replaces the depreciation in real value of past fixed-dollar investments produced by the accompanying inflation of prices (and provides, in addition, for some growth if the economy is expanding). They would regard the real revenue from deposit expansion as an additional return on a *given real stock* of assets and would attribute it to the higher nominal interest rates in the market resulting from anticipation of the accompanying inflation. Nevertheless, the two points of view are equivalent, as expressed by the two sides of the foregoing equation 12: $dD/Pdt = (D/P)\pi$, where π equals the amount of the change in the nominal rate of interest due to the anticipated rate of price change. On either view the revenue could be treated as income or as a recurring increase in net worth.

If the revenue is treated as income and paid to stockholders, net worth of banks on the balance sheet remains constant in real value while real dividends are paid at a higher rate. In real terms there is no addition to loanable funds; banks in effect use the real revenue from deposit expansion to pay higher real dividends. The process is exactly equivalent to one in which banks charge depositors a fee and transfer it to stockholders as dividend income. To pay the fee, depositors reduce real consumption and saving, and stockholders increase those expenditures. If the division between consumption and saving for each group is the same—and there is little basis for inferring how the owners of the bulk of deposits (mainly businesses) and of bank stock differ in this respect—total real saving is unchanged.

If the revenue is not paid to stockholders but retained to augment earning assets, net worth continually increases in real terms, and there is a corresponding rise in the real value of bank stock which is sooner or later reflected in its market value. A steady rise in real value of the stock represents imputed real income to stockholders. Stockholders can treat this like their other income and consume most of it by regularly selling an amount of stock equal to the continual rise in value. The sale of stock offsets the addition to real loanable funds of the bank expansion. Despite the sales, the stock retained continues to have the same total real value and, even though the real consumption expenditures of stockholders are commensurately higher, their net real wealth remains the same. Or as an alternative, they can reduce their real saving in other forms and continue to hold all the higher-valued bank stock.

Stockholders can thus offset the real loanable funds initially supplied by banks from the revenue of the inflation tax on money balances produced by an expansion of deposits. The economy provides for capital formation at the same rate as before, except that now part of the supply of loanable funds is furnished through the banking system instead of by stockholders through their saving of nonbank income. To illustrate, suppose that all consumers save one-tenth of income, and let us disregard possible changes in real deposit balances. Then depositors consume less in real terms by an amount equal to nine-tenths of deposit growth because of the accompanying inflation tax, and save less in real terms by one-tenth. Banks add to real loanable funds by an amount equal to the tax on deposits (assuming monetary reserves are zero; otherwise the result depends upon how the government disposes of its share, r, of the revenue, discussed below). Stockholders consume in real terms more by nine-tenths of the rising real value of bank stock due to the revenue from the tax; they hold the stock and cover the consumption by saving less in other forms. The rising value of bank stock should be included in their real net worth, which then grows by one-tenth of the tax. Total real loanable funds supplied are lower by one-tenth due to depositors, higher by one due to banks, and lower by nine-tenths due to stockholders; the net effect is zero.

Deposit expansion does not, therefore, add to net national saving unless stockholders regard the higher bank profits as temporary rather than permanent or as more uncertain than other sources of income, and treat these profits differently than depositors treat the tax imposed by the expansion. The argument is precisely the same as that, noted earlier, for the income to the beneficiaries of a franchise to issue currency. There are, however, two special qualifications here because deposits require non-interest-bearing reserves and have service costs.

Non-interest-bearing Reserves. A franchise to create deposits carries with it by law and custom an obligation to invest some fraction of the proceeds in a monetary reserve created independently of the private banking system, such as Treasury currency, central bank monetary liabilities, or specie, none of which pay interest. Reserve money might or might not have added, when first issued, to the supply of real loanable funds. It would not have, if it came into existence through an increase in government expenditures financed by reducing Treasury deposits at the central bank or through an expenditure of newly mined gold in goods or services. Reserve money might have augmented real loanable funds when first issued, if it came into existence through bond purchases by the central bank or by foreigners who converted their own currency into dollars at a fixed rate of exchange.[18] To the extent that reserves, when first issued, add to real loanable funds, deposit expansion reflects an issue of government money used to retire the national debt. Whether real saving increases depends, as discussed earlier, on how taxpayers respond to the decrease in the discounted value of future taxes which occurs because of lower interest on the national debt.

Costs of Servicing Deposits. Total expenses of banks are, for present purposes, of two kinds: One comprises the cost of making loans, acquiring assets, and providing a reserve for bad debts; these expenses may be deducted from gross earnings to derive net earnings on assets. The other expense covers the servicing of deposit accounts. When banks are expanding and prices rise to keep deposit balances in real terms the same, no resources to provide services on the new nominal deposits are necessary; the nominal service cost increases but the real cost remains unchanged. But, as the earlier analysis showed, an increase in the rate of change of prices induces banks to increase the level of services per deposit dollar, and for a system of banks the total cost of services $[s(D/P)]$ probably rises.

Banks meet increases in service costs out of the gross return on earning assets. Insofar as the increased services require equipment, banks will make a capital expenditure, financed by funds from their own capital or by borrowing on the open market. If an increase in deposit expansion leads to larger service costs, part of the newly created money will be used, in effect, to purchase additional equipment for banks. To that extent the new money, though initially used to acquire

---

[18] Insofar as foreign exchange or gold assets are a component of reserves for growing domestic money balances, the public may be viewed as "investing" in such assets in lieu of providing loanable funds for domestic capital formation.

financial assets, still does not augment the net supply of real loanable funds available to nonbank borrowers.

Insofar as increased services require additional clerks and tellers, banks commit themselves to a higher real payroll, which absorbs part of the return on the assets acquired in the expansion. To that extent the new money lent to borrowers is not absorbed by a lump-sum capital outlay by banks, and the supply of real loanable funds increases. What is the difference in principle between these payroll costs and those on bank equipment? Simply that newly hired labor requires no capital outlay. If additional labor were not available, the real wage rate would increase and induce more investment in human capital. Then the additional supply of loanable funds would again be absorbed, now by an induced increase in the demand to finance (human) capital. If idle bank equipment were available, it too could be leased and so would not require an initial outlay that absorbed the loanable funds produced by deposit expansion.

Summary.   When a bank creates deposits, it also acquires financial assets, but it does not necessarily add to the net supply of real loanable funds. The earnings on the assets are partly allocated to servicing deposits. Except when there are idle banking resources, provision of the services requires capital expenditures which to that extent absorb the new money. Any net profits of deposit creation go to the stockholders, who thus receive an increase either in real dividends or in the present market value of future profits to dispose of as they wish. If they increase their consumption expenditures to avoid what would otherwise be an unintended increase in their imputed real net worth, then there would be no increase in the net supply of loanable funds in real terms arising from money creation.

If a competitive banking system paid interest on demand deposits, the benefits of expansion (apart from monetary reserves) would go, as noted earlier, not to the stockholders, but to the depositors. The balance sheet of the banking system would remain unchanged in real terms; there would be no transfer of income from depositors to stockholders. Depositors would be compensated for the depreciating value of deposits to the full extent, except for the nonearning money reserves of banks. When inflation imposes a tax on money holders and the revenues are distributed to them, the same group pays the tax and collects the revenue, and therefore the tax has no real effect.

LAGS AND IMPERFECT FORESIGHT

All of the preceding analysis assumes that changes in monetary growth produce corresponding, fully anticipated effects on the rate of price increase. Let us consider two other situations. First, price increases are not anticipated, but nevertheless occur with no significant lag. Second, the economy is not at full employment, and monetary growth raises output but not prices. Redistributions of wealth due to usury laws or other restrictions on banks may also play a role but will be ignored.

If price increases are not anticipated, nominal interest rates do not rise to compensate for the depreciation in the real value of fixed-dollar assets. As a result, debtors receive unexpected gains and creditors unexpected losses in real terms. There is no net effect on real loanable funds, however, unless the two groups treat such gains and losses differently. It makes no difference that the price increases reflect an expansion of deposits via bank lending: The revenue in real terms from deposit expansion goes, not to the stockholders, but to bank borrowers who dispose of it as they wish.

To illustrate, let us start with the earlier example of fully anticipated price increases. There we first assumed that banks transferred the revenue from deposit expansion to stockholders as dividends. There was no addition to real loanable funds, because banks used the new deposits to make the higher dividend payments. Suppose now that price increases are not anticipated by anyone and nominal interest rates do not adjust. Banks no longer capture the revenue from deposit expansion, and it goes to their borrowers because of an unexpectedly lower real rate of interest. The only change in the example is that borrowers now receive a windfall in the form of a lower interest charge on loans in real terms, while in the previous case stockholders received higher dividends. No other difference is produced by the lack of anticipation of inflation, aside from redistributions of wealth. To be sure, banks are continually expanding deposits and loans in nominal terms, but in real terms their total loans outstanding remain the same because the added loans just compensate for the depreciation in the real value of outstanding loans. This depreciation is a capital loss to the bank equal to the value of new loans. Until old loans are repaid, a bank expansion can increase lending in real terms. But as loans are turned over, their reduced real value offsets the increase in real loanable funds due to the expansion.

A real effect on saving and the supply of loanable funds can come only from a different treatment of unexpected gains and losses by bank borrowers and depositors. It is not at all obvious what the net effect on aggregate real saving would be. It is true that the real rate of interest is lower, but that is unanticipated and so cannot itself affect borrowing and lending and nominal interest rates.

When the economy is not at full employment, monetary growth can increase real income. Suppose prices remain constant. There is still a revenue from money creation, but it is paid, not by an inflation tax on deposits, but by an increase in real deposits on the part of the recipients of the higher real incomes from the idle resources put to work. Part of the revenue is used to provide services on the larger real balances, and the remainder goes to bank stockholders directly as dividends or indirectly as a rise in net worth of banks.

It is, of course, unrealistic to assume that the beneficiaries of money creation act unhesitatingly and with complete foresight. The income from newly acquired bank assets will not be reflected immediately in the market value of bank stocks or in the services on deposits, and the consumption expenditures of the beneficiaries will not be adjusted rapidly. It takes time to see whether increased deposit growth will produce rising net income for stockholders or increased services for customers, and it is never clear how long any increase will last. Since the next quarter may well bring a reversal, seemingly transitory variations in imputed income hardly warrant an immediate rearrangement of consumption patterns. In that respect the creation of money by banks differs from a franchise given to a group of individuals to print money. The extent to which banks are able to use their franchise is variable and unpredictable. Because of their obligation to redeem deposits and other banking regulations, benefits to stockholders or depositors are slow and uncertain.

The lags and uncertainties suggest that money creation may well increase the supply of real loanable funds without being offset—contrary to the earlier argument—by the spending behavior of the ultimate beneficiaries of the new purchasing power. Stockholders may thus be led to "save" the imputed increase in their net worth. This addition to real loanable funds will not be offset by a reduction in real saving by depositors provided that the revenue reflects, not a tax on deposits imposed by rising prices, but, rather, a rise in real income which induces depositors to increase their real balances. Otherwise, if prices rise, depositors suffer a capital loss on deposits in real terms, and if they had not anticipated the loss we cannot be sure of their response, but it is quite possible that they would divert part of current saving to replenish the loss in real balances as a means of maintaining real balances at the desired level. This diversion of their saving would exactly offset the increased saving of stockholders.

The theoretical conditions for general credit effects on interest rates, therefore, are that deposit expansion not raise prices and that the resulting revenue be unanticipated or uncertain. These conditions are *least* likely to hold for constant rates of monetary growth, and *most* likely to hold for deviations of monetary growth from trend. Such effects are similar, in the economic behavior involved, to the muted response of consumption to transitory changes in receipts and payments. People resist making sharp changes in consumption and tend to even out variations in income by saving more when receipts exceed expected levels and by saving less or even dissaving when receipts fall short. This is also true for saving out of the imputed real income from money creation. Variations in monetary growth may produce inverse movements in interest rates, therefore, because real income and desired real balances are affected and the initial effect on the supply of loanable funds is not entirely offset by reduced real saving on the part of the beneficiaries of money creation.

3

The Statistical Association
Between Monetary Growth
and Interest Rates

This and the following two chapters investigate the empirical issues raised in the preceding chapter. In this chapter the relation between monetary growth and interest rates is examined, to see whether an inverse monetary effect can be found. The next two chapters present specific tests of the credit theory.

OVERVIEW OF THE TIME SERIES EVIDENCE

Short-run cycles in interest rates conform fairly closely to general business activity largely because of cyclical fluctuations in the total demand for credit. Interest rates do not conform perfectly, however, and many of the deviations are related to the rate of growth of the money stock. The relation is brought out by Chart 3-1, which shows the patterns of commercial paper rates and the rate of monetary growth over National Bureau reference cycles [1] since 1904. Money comprises commercial bank demand and time deposits and currency outside banks. Although the money series is available monthly only after May 1907, it was possible to extend the series with annual data

[1] Reference cycles are divided into nine stages; the terminal stage of one cycle and the initial stage of the next are the same. Trough (I and IX) and peak (V) stages are averages of the three months surrounding the reference trough and peak months, respectively. Stages II–IV divide the period from trough to peak into thirds, and stages VI–VII divide the contraction phase into thirds.

CHART 3-1

Nonwar Cyclical Patterns of Commercial Paper Rate and Monetary Growth Rate, Reference Cycle Stages, 1904–69

(numerical deviations from cycle averages)

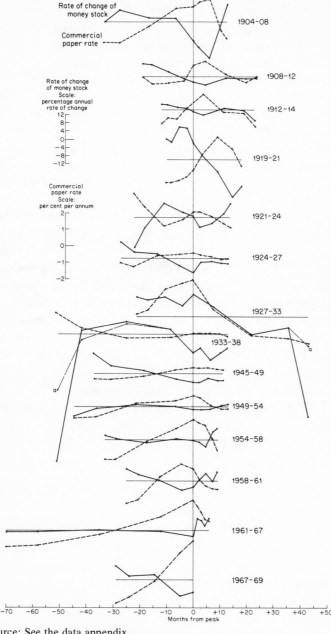

Source: See the data appendix.

a Including unlicensed banks, 1933–34.

to cover all stages of the 1904–08 cycle. One and a half additional cycles beyond 1961 were constructed by hypothesizing a business peak in December 1966, when industrial production began a moderate decline; a trough in June 1967, when production turned sharply upward; and a peak in November 1969. The 1967 contraction in business seems too small and too short to qualify as a full-fledged downturn, but it has the earmarks of a borderline recession.

The chart reveals a negative association between the two series, particularly in their deviations from general business activity in the timing of peaks and troughs. Many turning points in commercial paper rates came much later than the reference turn, and the lagged timing was often associated with a similar discrepancy in the corresponding inverse turn of the monetary growth rate. The frequent occurrence of corresponding *deviations* provides strong support of a direct link between the variables.

The inverse association is far from perfect, to be sure. The largest exceptions, however, reflect special episodes: the short contraction phase of the World War I cycle, when monetary growth declined erratically from the high wartime levels (in part because the stages were relatively short, which emphasizes the volatility of the monthly changes); and the severe 1929–33 contraction in business, when short-term interest rates and high-grade bond yields fell despite sharp declines in monetary growth. The 1929–33 episode may be explained by the financial crisis: Banks and the public sold risky assets to acquire high-grade securities and money. Potential borrowers with prime ratings tried to avoid incurring debt. In consequence, rates on prime commercial loans and high-grade securities fell sharply while medium- and low-grade bond yields rose. The standard money figures exclude banks not licensed to reopen immediately after the 1933 panic and so overstate the reduction in the money stock appropriately defined.[2] For the affected stages, the chart also shows the money stock adjusted to include the deposits in unlicensed banks. The adjustment lessens the exceptional nature of that period.

The extreme observations on the chart should not draw attention away from the association prevailing in ordinary periods. It is apt to

[2] See Milton Friedman and Anna Schwartz, *A Monetary History of the United States, 1867–1960*, Princeton for NBER, 1963, pp. 422–33.

be overlooked because of other distracting movements in the series owing to the strong influence on interest rates of other economic variables. Three statistical difficulties summarize the problems of sub-stantiating the association: First, the volatility of the monthly rate of change of the money stock requires smoothing in some way to bring out its intermediate-run association with interest rates. Second, interest rates exhibit long-run swings lasting fifteen to thirty years or longer which should be distinguished from cyclical movements. Third, these variables have similar cyclical fluctuations, which can produce the appearance of correlation between them even though they may not be directly interrelated.

The use of reference cycle stages helps to overcome these difficul-ties and to isolate the association. Averaging the data for reference stages substantially reduces the volatility in the monthly rate of change of money. The stage averages sharply reduce the number of observa-tions otherwise available from monthly data, but not more than seems desirable to avoid the high serial dependence in monthly time series. If we take changes between stages, the long-run movements in the data are largely eliminated, allowing the analysis to focus on the short-run relation between the series. Chart 3-2 presents a scatter diagram of the stage-to-stage changes of the series in Chart 3-1 through the 1966 peak. (Later stages were not available when this chart and the subsequent statistical analysis were done.)

Reference cycle stages may be viewed as an irregular transformation of the time scale to reduce autocorrelation and short-run random fluctuations. The linear transformation produced by quarterly or semi-annual averages would be conceptually simpler, but would not get at the main problem. Usually the most common source of spurious corre-lation between economic series apart from trend is cyclical fluctuations. A time unit based on the duration of cyclical stages makes it much easier to determine whether two series are correlated solely because of their tendency to rise and fall with business activity. One indication of such spurious correlation between two series is a sharp decline in cor-relation when they are converted into deviations from average ref-erence cycle patterns. That decline does not occur here, however, as is shown in the next chapter by the use of dummy variables for each stage change to take account of the average cyclical pattern.

CHART 3-2

Monetary Growth Rate and Commercial Paper Rate, Changes Between
Successive Reference Cycle Stages (Special Periods Dated), 1904–66

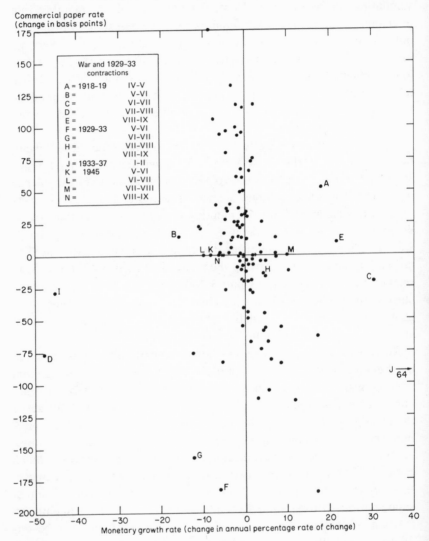

    Source: See the data appendix (same as Chart 3-1; not adjusted for unlicensed banks,
1933–35).

To be sure, reference stage averages are a crude way to eliminate spurious correlation. Ideally, it would be better to include in the regression other variables which account for part of the common fluctuations in the other two. But there are not always satisfactory proxies for these other variables, while the reference cycle is a handy substitute, easy to apply and to interpret. The stage averages also act as a weighting scheme for time series, giving the highest weight to movements covering a cyclical stage and the lowest to movements very short relative to reference stages. This seems preferable to treating each month as equally significant. No doubt the weighting scheme could be improved,[3] but it seems adequate to bring out the relation over business cycles between monetary growth and interest rates. In the appendix to this chapter, the purposes and consequences of averaging the data by reference stages are discussed.

REGRESSION ANALYSIS

To demonstrate the statistical significance of the association, Table 3-1 presents correlation coefficients between the monetary growth rate and various interest rates. The series for the top panel are first differences of reference stage averages, as in Chart 3-2. That is, the monthly *level* of the interest rates and the month-to-month *percentage change* in the money stock, both seasonally adjusted, were first averaged for reference stages. The changes between these successive stage averages were then used in the regressions. The interest series are market rates on prime commercial paper of four to six months, on Treasury notes and certificates of three to six months before 1929, linked to Treasury bills of three months thereafter (full series referred to here simply as Treasury bills), on bank loans (an average of varying coverage), on long-term U.S. bonds, on high-grade corporate and municipal bonds (Standard and Poor's), on Macaulay's adjusted average of railroad bonds, and on low-grade

---

[3] In particular, it would be preferable to use stages of equal length for each complete phase, and not shorter ones for troughs and peaks as here, though the results from omitting these stages made little difference. A more sophisticated refinement might be to vary the length of stages according to the time span of autocorrelation in the data.

TABLE 3-1

Relation Between Interest Rates and Monetary Growth Rate,
Various Periods, 1868–1966

Interest Rate and Period	Correlation Coefficient	t Value [a]
	Changes Between Reference Cycle Stages [b]	
1919–66		
Commercial paper	−.42	3.9
Treasury bills	−.44	4.1
U.S. bonds	−.45	4.3
Corporate and municipal bonds	−.16	1.4
1919–61		
Bank loans —	−.40	3.6
Low-grade bonds	−.38	3.5
	Annual Changes [c]	
Commercial paper		
1868–1914	−.55	4.4
1919–66	−.67	5.4
Treasury bills		
1920–66	−.57	4.0
U.S. bonds		
1919–66	−.47	3.2
Railroad bonds		
1868–1914	−.25	1.7
Corporate and municipal bonds		
1919–66	−.48	3.2

Source: See the data appendix.

[a] Signs of t values, which pertain to the regression coefficient and are all negative, have been omitted. $t \geq 2.0$ is significant at the .05 level.

[b] Changes between nine successive reference-cycle stage averages of monthly interest rates (for bank loans, quarterly data after 1938) and of month-to-month percentage change in money stock.

For all regressions, except with low-grade bonds, coverage excludes changes between stages V and IX of 1914–18 and 1938–45 war contractions and between V and II of the 1929–33 contraction and subsequent revival (to omit the 1933 trough stage); with bank loans, coverage also excludes stage changes I–II and II–III of the 1938–45 expansion (because of a break in the series). With low-grade bonds, only stages VIII–IX of 1927–33 and I–II of the 1933–38 cycles are excluded to omit the extreme decline in money stock in March 1933. Treasury bill series begins with the peak stage of the 1919–21 cycle; bank loans and U.S. and Baa bonds begin with the initial trough stage of that cycle. Bank loans and low-grade bonds end with the 1961 trough; others, with the assumed peak in 1966.

[c] Year-to-year change in interest rates (fiscal-year average of monthly data) and June-to-June percentage change in money stock, excluding 1930–33 and 1940–46.

bonds (Moody's Baa average). Sources are given in the data appendix.

The 1929–33 contraction and the two war contractions of 1918–19 and 1945 are the source of the extreme observations lettered in Chart 3-2; they distort the over-all association between monetary growth and interest rates and have been excluded in Table 3-1. Unlike the other series, yields on low-grade bonds rose in the 1929–33 contraction, and that period was *not* excluded in the regression for that series. When 1929–33 and the war contractions are included for the other rate series, the correlation (not shown) is reduced, but it is still significant. The adjustment to include unlicensed banks 1933–34 was not used for the regressions.

To indicate whether the reference-stage averages produce quite special results, the bottom panel of the table gives corresponding correlations using changes in annual data, that is, the average monthly level of the interest rates for fiscal years and the June-to-June percentage change in the money stock were converted to first differences – year-to-year changes – for use in the regressions. The Great Depression and World War II (1930–33 and 1940–46) were excluded.[4] The results in the two panels of the table are similar.

Although not large, the correlation coefficients in Table 3-1 are on the whole highly significant. Most interest rates exhibit similar short-run movements; if monetary growth correlates with one series, it will correlate with all of them, though the correlation tends to be higher for rates on commercial paper and U.S. securities than for the others. High coefficients are not to be expected, simply because the regressions omit all the nonmonetary factors affecting financial markets. Monetary growth accounts for 3 to 44 per cent – typically about 25 per cent – of the cyclical variation in interest rates, depending on the interest rate and the period. (This range corresponds to correlation coefficients of between .16 and .67.)

The remainder of this variation in interest rates can be attributed to other supply and demand factors. These would be difficult to identify and measure, but many of them were clearly associated with the business cycle, as is shown by adding to the previous regressions a proxy or dummy variable to represent movements in general business ac-

[4] The regressions for bank loans and low-grade bonds were computed before the data after 1961 became available.

tivity. Several such proxies for demand influences (industrial production, personal income, gross national product) were experimented with. The partial correlation coefficients of these variables with interest rates (not shown) were all highly significant and positive, suggesting the strong influence of cycles on the demand for loanable funds. (Supply factors with positive conformity to business cycles would tend to produce negative coefficients.) These proxies were only slightly correlated with the money variable, however (partly because the series have been expressed as first differences); consequently, their inclusion had little effect on the correlation found between monetary growth and interest rates.

A few unusually large observations can sometimes account for most of an observed correlation. Omitting all the stage changes with extreme values of the money series, however, made little difference. The regressions with those exclusions are presented in Table 3-2 for reference stage changes. Column 1 shows the correlations omitting just the 1929–33 and war contractions. The coefficients differ slightly from those in Table 3-1 for the corresponding interest rates because Table 3-1 was based on a later revised version of the money series and excludes stages I and II of the 1933–38 cycle, included here in column 1. Also, Table 3-2 excludes the stages after 1961 (not available at the time of computation) and includes the years 1904 to World War I for those interest-rate series which were available for that period.

Column 2 excludes seven other observations with extremely large rates of monetary growth or decline; the results are practically the same. When we also omit the period of unusually low interest rates after 1933 and the subsequent pegging of rates by the Federal Reserve from 1942 to the early 1950s (column 3), the correlation is even higher.

It can be argued that time deposits at commercial banks should be excluded from the money series. The argument based on the credit theory would be that, if they are a closer substitute for savings bank deposits than for demand deposits, the addition to total credit supplied by commercial banks when they gain time deposits will usually be largely offset by a decrease in credit supplied by other financial intermediaries losing deposits. Hence an expansion of time deposits does not augment the net supply of credit by an equal amount. The portfolio

TABLE 3-2

Correlation Coefficients Between Interest Rates and Monetary Growth Rate, Changes Between Reference Cycle Stages, Various Periods, 1904–61

Interest Rate and Period	Period Covered Excluding		
	War Contrac- tions and 1929–33 (1)	Other Stages with Extreme Values [a] (2)	1919–29 and 1953–61 Only (3)
	Including Time Deposits in Money Series		
Commercial paper, 1904–61	−.47	−.48	−.56
Treasury bills, 1920–61 [b]	−.46	−.48	−.61
Bank loans, 1919–61	−.46	−.38	−.51
U.S. bonds, 1919–61	−.42	−.42	−.47
Corp. and municipal bonds, 1904–61	−.38	−.43	−.39
	Excluding Time Deposits From Money Series [c]		
Commercial paper, 1914–61	−.38	−.44	−.49
Treasury bills, 1920–61 [b]	−.40	−.43	−.52
U.S. bonds, 1919–61	−.36	−.39	−.40
Corp. and municipal bonds, 1914–61	−.32	−.36	−.32

Source and coverage: Same as for Table 3-1, except that all regressions end with 1961 trough, and some begin earlier.

[a] Excluded stage changes: 1904–08, VII–VIII; 1914–19, I–II and IV–V; 1919–21, VII–VIII; 1921–24, II–III; and 1933–38, I–II and IV–V; as well as those noted for column 1.

[b] Excluding the 1919–20 expansion stages; not available for Treasury bill rate.

[c] Not computed for bank loans.

theory argument would be that time deposits may not be a part of money balances.

The sharp fluctuation in growth of time deposits during the 1960s because of deposit-rate ceilings argues for their exclusion. But earlier periods are a different matter. During the 1920s and 1930s, differences in the relative growth of demand and time deposits reflected shifts between them by the public on a large scale.[5] Excluding time deposits then would misrepresent the net changes in funds commercial banks supplied to the credit market. Also, before the 1930s some time deposits could be transferred by check and were not clearly distinguished from demand deposits.

It is difficult to settle this question by time series regressions for the period covered here. Some slight support for including time deposits is provided by correlation coefficients (bottom panel of Table 3-2) for which time deposits were excluded (the data, however, cover just the post-1914 period, when time and demand deposits could be separated in the monthly data). The exclusion of time deposits lowers the correlation, though, as expected, only slightly and not significantly.

AN ALTERNATIVE INTERPRETATION OF THE ASSOCIATION

The preceding evidence supports the view that changes in the rate of monetary growth affect interest rates. Before accepting this interpretation, however, we should examine the possibility of an influence running in the opposite direction, in which interest-rate movements produce changes in the money stock.

Interest rates can affect monetary growth in various ways which might account for the observed correlation and contradict the preceding interpretation. The importance of such effects can be assessed by examining the relation between interest rates and the principal sources of change in the money stock, namely, the actions of the federal government, the banks, and the public.[6] Attributing money-stock changes to the influence of these sectors is traditional.[7] Therefore, the derivation of a formula for measuring these influences need be sketched here only briefly.

The federal government is responsible for changes in high-powered money, H (the monetary base which serves partly as bank reserves

[5] Discussed in Phillip Cagan, *Determinants and Effects of Changes in the Stock of Money, 1875–1960*, New York, NBER, 1965, pp. 171–73.

[6] Time deposits are included throughout this section.

[7] See, for example, Friedman and Schwartz, *Monetary History*, App. B; and Cagan, *Determinants and Effects*, Chap. 1.

and partly as circulating hand-to-hand currency, and consists of currency, Federal Reserve deposit liabilities, and, before 1934, gold outside the Treasury). The money stock publicly held, M, equals currency outside banks, C, plus commercial bank deposits, D; $M \equiv C + D$. High-powered money outstanding that is not held as currency by the public is held by banks as reserves, R; $H \equiv C + R$. From these definitions it follows that

$$M \equiv \frac{H}{(C/M) + (R/D) - (C/M)(R/D)}$$

in which the money stock depends on high-powered money issued by the monetary authorities (the Treasury and Federal Reserve banks), the currency ratio of the public, C/M, and the reserve ratio of banks, R/D. High-powered money affects the money stock positively, while the two ratios have inverse effects. Writing both sides in terms of natural logarithms and differentiating with respect to time gives, after collecting terms,

$$\frac{d \ln M}{dt} \equiv \frac{d \ln H}{dt} + \frac{M}{H}\left(1 - \frac{R}{D}\right)\frac{d(-C/M)}{dt} + \frac{M}{H}\left(1 - \frac{C}{M}\right)\frac{d(-R/D)}{dt}$$

$$m \equiv h + c + r.$$

In this form, the rate of change of the money stock is the sum of three parts representing changes in high-powered money, the currency ratio, and the reserve ratio. Here r denotes the contribution of the reserve ratio to monetary growth (not, as in Chapter 2, the reserve ratio itself). The derivatives may be approximated by discrete monthly changes. This introduces a slight error, since the three parts do not then add exactly to the total rate of monetary growth. However, the approximation is close enough for practical purposes.

The correlation between interest rates and the monetary growth rate implies, by the foregoing identity, a correlation between interest rates and the three sources of the growth rate. Different theories of the direction of influence, however, imply different relations between interest rates and each of the three sources. If interest-rate effects are largely responsible for the inverse association with monetary growth, the effects on the three sources should be in different directions. A rise in interest rates tends to reduce the reserve ratio and therefore to increase the money stock. A rise in interest rates also tends to reduce the public's desire to hold currency, and thus also to increase the money stock. To be sure, such effects are limited; hence higher interest rates would be expected to raise the *growth rate* of the money stock only temporarily. Nevertheless, we still expect the main effect on the rate of change to be positive or zero.

The above formulation treats member bank borrowing from the Federal Reserve as part of the contribution of high-powered money, on the grounds that the volume of such borrowing is taken into account and offset by the monetary authorities in conducting open-market operations. Another point of view looks upon borrowed reserves as determined by member banks and implicitly disregards any offset by open-market operations. The preceding identity can incorporate this second view, if reserves borrowed by member banks are excluded from high-powered money and subtracted from bank reserves. (The subtraction from reserves in excess of requirements gives the free reserves of banks, which are always less than excess money reserves and often negative.) Even on this formulation, interest rates are still expected to affect monetary growth positively. A well-known study of free reserves [8] argues that a rise in interest rates (relative to the discount rate at which member banks can borrow from the Federal Reserve) lowers the desired level of free reserves and makes the actual level temporarily too high. To close the gap, banks step up their rate of expansion of earning assets. The result is to produce a positive association between interest rates and the rate of deposit growth.

Given these positive effects, the observed *negative* correlation between interest rates and monetary growth suggests two alternative explanations. Either (1) interest rates have a sufficiently strong negative effect on the contribution to monetary growth of the unborrowed portion of high-powered money to overcome their positive effect on the other sources, or (2) the negative correlation between interest rates and monetary growth should be attributed largely to monetary effects, interest effects on monetary growth being relatively minor.

Table 3-3 presents correlation coefficients of interest rates with each

[8] A. J. Meigs, *Free Reserves and the Money Supply*, Chicago, University of Chicago Press, 1962.

TABLE 3-3

Correlation Coefficients Between Sources of Monetary Growth and Interest Rates, Changes Between Reference Cycle Stages, Various Periods, 1904–61

Contribution to Monetary Growth Rate [a]	Period Covered Excluding		1919–29 and 1953–61 Only
	War Contractions and 1929–33 (1)	Other Stages with Extreme Values [b] (2)	(3)
	Commercial Paper Rate, 1904–61		
h_t	.08	.06	−.14
h_u	−.06		
c	−.39 *	−.25 *	−.24
r	−.13	−.18	−.16
	Treasury Bill Rate, 1920–61 [c]		
h_t	−.10	−.05	.00
h_u	−.05		
c	−.29 *	−.33 *	−.40 *
r	−.13	−.16	−.22
	U.S. Bond Rate, 1919–61		
h_t	−.11	−.02	−.05
h_u	.02		
c	−.10	−.11	−.33 *
r	−.25 *	−.27 *	−.12
	Corporate and Municipal Bond Rate, 1904–61		
h_t	−.05	−.02	−.06
h_u	−.01		
c	−.17	−.09	−.23
r	−.18	−.22	−.10

Source: Same as for Table 3-2, with time deposits included. Member bank borrowing from *Banking and Monetary Statistics* and *Federal Reserve Bulletin*.

[a] The contributions to the rate of monetary growth are h_t for high-powered money, h_u for h_t excluding member bank borrowing, c for the currency ratio, and r for the reserve ratio.

[b] Same exclusions as for Table 3-2.

[c] Excluding 1919–20 expansion stages, which are not available for Treasury bill rate.

* Significant at the .05 level.

of these sources of monetary growth. The contribution of high-powered money is shown both in total (h_t) and with member bank borrowing excluded (h_u). To be comparable with Table 3-2, the observations are changes between reference cycle stages and cover the same periods. The coefficients do not reveal a strong negative relation between interest rates and the rate of change of high-powered money either including or excluding borrowing, contrary to the first explanation above. Indeed, those coefficients are virtually zero.

Most of the correlation with the contributions of the two ratios is negative, though generally not significant. This cannot reflect the response of bank reserves and the public's currency holdings to interest-rate movements, because in theory their contribution to monetary growth should have a positive association with interest rates. (Remember that the signs of changes in the currency and reserve ratios are reversed in measuring their contributions to growth in the money stock.) Although the table does not include the free reserve ratio, in theory its relation here to interest rates should also be positive. These contributions cannot, therefore, account for the much higher negative correlation between interest rates and the growth rate of the total money stock. The negative correlations in the table apparently reflect the opposite direction of influence, in which the separate sources, acting through the total money stock, affect interest rates.[9]

It might be argued that, if the Federal Reserve persistently and successfully pursued a policy of controlling total high-powered money so as to make the monetary growth rate move inversely to interest rates, the observed correlation could be produced, even though monetary growth had no effect on interest rates and even though interest rates showed little or no association with each of the three sources of monetary growth. In that case much of the movement in high-powered money would have been devoted to offsetting fluctuations in the currency and reserve ratios. Since the two ratios were not themselves influenced by interest rates, high-powered money might

---

[9] My study "Interest Rates and the Reserve Ratio: A Reinterpretation of the Statistical Association," in Jack M. Guttentag and Phillip Cagan (eds.), *Essays on Interest Rates,* New York, NBER, 1969, Vol. I, confirms a negative effect of interest rates on the free reserve ratio, but a much weaker one than usually reported if loan demand is held constant. Even then, fluctuations in the free reserve ratio are not large, and the effect of interest rates on deposit growth through this channel appears to be negligible.

not show an inverse association with interest rates. Reserve officials, for example, might have regarded a steep rise in interest rates as evidence of an overheated economy and taken steps to reduce monetary growth, in the process offsetting contrary movements in the currency and reserve ratios, and, conversely, for declines in interest rates.

But this implies that Federal Reserve policy was guided primarily by interest rates and was intended to reinforce their movements, whereas in fact they often tried to moderate them. That the Federal Reserve consistently followed such a limited guide is hardly credible in view of the variety of policies it actually pursued over the years.[10]

Moreover, the negative association between monetary growth and interest rates for the period 1868–1914 (Table 3-1) must run from money to the rates, since there was then no central bank authority to control the money supply nor any mechanism to make it *inversely* responsive to interest rates. The same correlation in the post-1914 period cannot plausibly be given a contrary interpretation.

CONCLUSIONS

The evidence points to an inverse effect of monetary growth on interest rates. The effect is not overpowering, and volatility in the money series and other strong influences on interest rates tend to hide it. But it appears not to be a spurious reflection of the common influence of business cycles on the variables or an effect of interest rates on the amount of money supplied. The most plausible inference is that changes in the growth rate of the money stock shift the supply curve of loanable funds and produce inverse movements in interest

---

[10] Other recent work on the supply of money reaches the same conclusion. Regressions of Federal Reserve credit supplied to the market show that it is related to a variety of variables and that interest rates actually have a small *positive* effect. See John H. Wood, "A Model of Federal Reserve Behavior," in G. Horwich (ed.), *Monetary Process and Policy: A Symposium*, Homewood, Ill., R. D. Irwin, 1967, pp. 135–66.

Similarly, in studies of the effect of aggregate expenditures on the money supply, this feedback is found to be weak. See Leonall C. Andersen, "Additional Empirical Evidence on the Reverse-Causation Argument," Federal Reserve Bank of St. Louis *Review*, August 1969, pp. 19–23. See also David I. Fand, "Some Implications of Money Supply Analysis," *American Economic Review*, May 1967. I made a similar argument in *Determinants and Effects*, pp. 273–75.

rates. That proposition in various forms has long been a part of monetary theory. Two theories to explain this association are tested in the next chapter.

APPENDIX: THE USE OF REFERENCE CYCLE STAGES IN REGRESSION ANALYSIS

Cycles in general business activity impart fluctuations to nearly all economic time series. From trough to trough or from peak to peak the cycles vary in duration from two to five years or so. Such fluctuations pose two problems for regression analysis. First of all, the assumption of standard regression analysis that the residual error term is random or serially independent usually does not hold. The main reason is that regression equations are rough approximations of complex market behavior and disregard numerous influences which are difficult to measure or are thought to be of secondary importance. The residual term incorporates the omitted variables, which usually contain cyclical fluctuations. Such fluctuations produce serial correlation. Also, even some of the included variables may be only proxies for other hard-to-measure variables, which have cyclical fluctuations not perfectly reproduced in the proxies. As a result, the error term is not random over time but contains the difference between the cyclical fluctuation in the proxy and the omitted variables. For these reasons the residual term typically is autocorrelated in time series regressions. First differences and models of the autocorrelated disturbance can be introduced to remove the serial dependence in the error term. By the Durbin-Watson statistic and other tests, these procedures are generally successful, though their appropriateness can be questioned, since the implicit assumption of these procedures is that two successive error terms are linearly related. Actually, they are more likely to be related by a sinusoidal function of varying periodicity.

In any event, autocorrelation in the residuals and methods to eliminate it are not likely to pose disabling obstacles unless precise estimates of the regression coefficients are needed. Usually we only want to test the significance of a relationship and the direction of certain effects.

A second problem is in my view more serious: Cycles in the included independent variables can serve as proxy for similar cycles in omitted variables. Then a spuriously high correlation can be obtained even though the equation is misspecified and some crucial variables are omitted from it. The similar cyclical fluctuations in economic time series make such spurious correlation between the dependent and each independent variable a common occurrence. Treatment of the error term for autocorrelation does not help here; indeed, it may remove fluctuations from the error term and lead us to infer that autocorrelation is absent when in fact the omission of certain variables means that it should be present.

It seems desirable, therefore, to test all questionable time series regressions for the influence of common cyclical fluctuations. It is not that relationships observed in the form of cyclical fluctuations are not meaningful; they are—if the correlation indeed reflects the particular influence that the regression is designed to measure. Many economic variables correlate with each other, however, solely because of common cyclical patterns. If two variables are genuinely related to each other, they should display related movements which are not a common reflection of cycles in general business activity.

Averages of the data for stages of reference cycles can be used to highlight common cyclical fluctuations in the data. The average has the advantage of smoothing out very short-run fluctuations in the data. What remains are trend and intermediate-run movements. Trends can be removed by taking first differences of the stage averages.

The effect of stage averages on a trendless series which conforms perfectly to reference cycles of varying lengths is illustrated in Figure 3-1. The figure was drawn on the assumption that the varying length of the phases stretches or squeezes the horizontal shape of the curve but does not change its average amplitude. Consequently, when we average by stages, dividing each phase into trough, peak, and three equal intervening stages, the curve has the same general shape in every expansion and contraction. Any series affected by business cycles in this way will show after the averaging a very similar pattern for every cycle.

The effect of taking first differences of the stage averages is illustrated at the bottom of Figure 3-1. Evenly spaced first differences of a triangular pattern would yield a step function: a constant positive value during the expansions and constant negative value during the contrac-

FIGURE 3-1

Transformation of a Trendless, Perfectly Conforming Linear Series
into Reference Cycle Patterns

Hypothetical Original Series

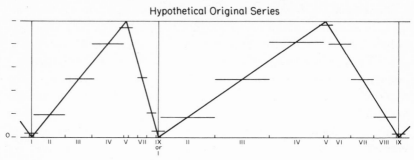

Reference Cycle Stage Averages

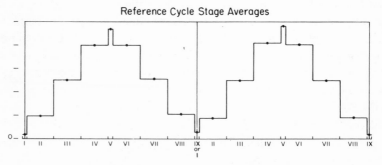

First Differences of Reference Cycle Pattern

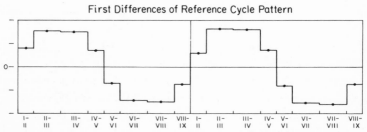

tions, with steps at the turning points. The first differences of stage averages are not evenly spaced, however. Trough and peak stages overlap the adjacent stages, and the stages within each phase differ by one month when the number of months within the phase is not divisible by three. As a result, the first differences resemble a somewhat jagged curve more than a step pattern. Nevertheless, the first differences have no trend and transform a smooth, perfectly conforming series into a succession of symmetrical and very similar cyclical patterns, even if the slope of the original series flattens out in longer phases and steepens in shorter ones.

In a regression where the economic variables are in the form of changes between successive reference cycle stages, dummy variables can be added to absorb the common cyclical fluctuations in the economic variables (this technique is used in Chapter 4). Seven dummy variables are added to the regression equation, one for each stage-to-stage change but the last (to avoid overdetermining the regression). For each stage change, the corresponding dummy variable is unity and the other six are zero. This is equivalent to fitting the regressions without dummies to the data for the stage change I–II separately, II–III separately, and so on for each of the eight stage changes, under the condition that the regression coefficients be the same for all fits.

The dummies in effect hold constant the regular cyclical fluctuation. What is not held constant are deviations from this pattern, including responses to the business cycle which vary in timing or amplitude from cycle to cycle or occur over time at a rate not in proportion to the duration of the concurrent reference phase. Two variables may be highly correlated in a simple regression, but when we hold the common cyclical component constant they will not be correlated unless the irregular cyclical movements are related.

The stage averages allow each stage equal influence on the regression fit, no matter how long the actual period of time covered by the stage. Thus, long expansions, which would otherwise contribute many more observations than short ones, carry no extra weight. Although unusually long phases have been infrequent before 1961, ordinary expansions were still two to four times longer than most contractions. The disadvantage of calendar time weighting is that a long, comparatively smooth business expansion tends to induce trendlike movements in most economic variables, which then appear to be correlated with each other even though their behavior is otherwise dissimilar. The largely unidirectional movements of variables during reference expansions receive much more weight on a calendar time scale than do the often sharp but short movements during reference contractions. With stage averages the movements in the two phases receive equal weight, though if it is desired, they could be weighted in some other way.

Reference cycle averages, therefore, are a desirable supplement to standard calendar time data, but not a substitute. There are obvious disadvantages to the stage changes: They may suppress some relevant short-run movements; they may give too much weight to relatively short and erratic movements in contractions, when errors of measurement may be relatively large; and they cannot be used for lag patterns unless the length of the lags varies with the duration of the business cycle phases. To check on these possible drawbacks of reference stage data, annual or monthly regressions have been used in this study to supplement the stage changes and to estimate lags.

4

A Test of the Credit and
Portfolio Effects

DEFINITION OF CREDIT AND MONEY

According to the credit theory of money, the growth of bank credit, for which growth of the total money stock is simply a good proxy, is the source of monetary effects on interest rates. The test presented in this chapter is based upon distinguishing the contribution of an expansion of credit from that of other components of monetary growth. Regression analysis is then used to estimate their separate effects on interest rates.

On the consolidated balance sheet of the monetary system, credit is represented by net earning assets—funds lent to the public. Currency issues and deposits are monetary liabilities. For individual banks, changes in total credit and deposits are closely related, though not identical because other items enter the two sides of the balance sheet. In the aggregate, changes in the money stock and in the net earning assets of banks and the government are generally not closely related.

Table 4-1 shows how the credit items are related to the money stock in a condensed balance sheet. Nonfinancial assets and liabilities are omitted. The money stock in the hands of the public comprises deposits with commercial banks (16) plus currency outside banks (lines $6 + 9 - 13$).[1] Credit supplied to the public by the monetary system is represented by net earning assets (lines $2 + 14 + 15 - 10$). In a com-

---

[1] The minor amount of Treasury currency in vaults of Federal Reserve banks can be treated as a deduction from Federal Reserve notes outstanding.

plete consolidation of the Federal Reserve and the Treasury with commercial banks, certain items cancel: loans to banks (3 and 19), member bank reserves (4 and 11), interbank deposits (12 and 17), and Treasury deposits (7 and 8 against 5 and 18). The remaining item

TABLE 4-1

Condensed Balance Sheet of Monetary and Credit Items of Federal Reserve Banks, U.S. Treasury, and Commercial Banks

Assets	Liabilities
A. Federal Reserve Banks	
1. Gold reserve	Deposits of:
Earning assets:	4. Commercial banks
2. Securities	5. U.S. Treasury
3. Loans to banks	6. Net Federal Reserve notes outstanding
B. U.S. Treasury	
Deposits with:	
7. Federal Reserve Banks	9. Net currency outstanding [a]
8. Commercial banks	10. Securities outside government agencies
C. Commercial Banks	
Deposits with:	Deposits (less bank float) of:
11. Federal Reserve Banks	16. Public
12. Other commercial banks	17. Other commercial banks
13. Vault cash	18. U.S. Treasury
Earning assets:	19. Due to Federal Reserve banks
14. Loans	
15. Investments	

Monetary liabilities = 6 + 9 − 13 + 16
Net earning assets
   Consolidated monetary system = 2 + 14 + 15 − 10
   Banking system excluding Treasury = 2 + 14 + 15
     Federal Reserve banks   = 2 + 3
     Commercial banks   = 14 + 15 − 19

[a] Including note liabilities of national banks before the notes were retired in 1935.

shown, the gold reserve (1), represents the reserves of the monetary system under the international gold standard.

The money stock and net earning assets are not identical. The difference is due not only to the noncanceling gold reserve but also to the numerous nonfinancial items not shown. Thus, gold flows stem from the international payments mechanism, only part of which entails debt issue; Treasury deposits help absorb short-run discrepancies between federal budget receipts and expenditures and trust funds, whose operations only in part involve credit transactions with the public; and other liabilities of the banking system represent a miscellany of operations which can affect the money stock and earning assets differently.

Loans made by the Treasury under various federal programs are not included in the credit total. Such loans are treated as though they were ordinary expenditures, as many of them are. In recent years Treasury lending has increased sharply through such agencies as the Federal National Mortgage Association (which was made a private corporation outside the federal budget in 1968). Fortunately, they are not important for the period covered here, and their exclusion can be passed over.

The Treasury could be excluded altogether (except for adding Treasury currency—line 9—to Federal Reserve notes—line 6); the effect of that alternative treatment will be discussed later. But deducting Treasury securities outstanding—line 10—from the earning assets of the banking system seems desirable in order to allow for transactions between the Treasury and the banking system which have no effect on the public. For example, if the Treasury sells a bond to commercial banks and deposits the proceeds in one of its commercial bank accounts, the money stock and the borrowing of the public are unaffected by the bookkeeping of this transaction; yet investments and the total credit of banks have increased. If we deduct Treasury securities outstanding, however, total credit available to the public is unchanged, as is proper. A similar example could be given involving bond transactions between the Treasury and the Federal Reserve.

In this treatment of Treasury debt operations, it is also true that a budget deficit financed by selling bonds to the public reduces total credit available to the public without affecting the money stock. Such

CHART 4-1

Reference Cycle Patterns of Growth in the Money Stock and in Net Earning Assets of the Consolidated Monetary System, 1948–66

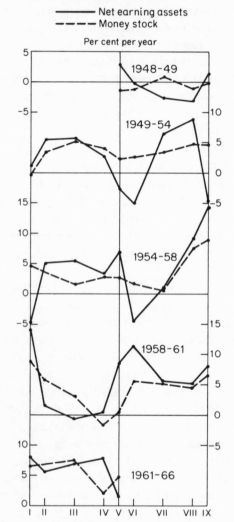

Source: Data appendix. For definition of variables, see Table 4-1.

debt operations contribute to differences between changes in money and in credit.

Chart 4-1 shows reference cycle patterns of monthly changes in net earning assets and the money stock as defined above, both expressed as percentages of the money stock. The chart covers the period since

CHART 4-2

Comparison of Growth in the Money Stock and in Net
Earning Assets of the Consolidated Monetary System,
Changes Between Reference Cycle Stages, 1948–66
(change in per cent per year)

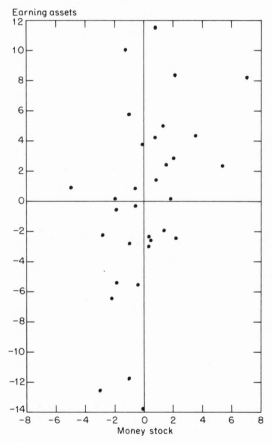

Source: Data appendix. For definition of variables, see Table 4-1.

1948 for which monthly data for all commercial banks are available. The patterns are certainly highly similar, as we might expect, but the movements are not identical. The degree of covariation is shown by Chart 4-2, a scatter diagram of the stage-to-stage changes in each series. The correlation coefficient for the scatter is .42, indicative of considerable divergence. This shows that it is possible to distinguish the two variables statistically.

REGRESSION TEST OF THE TWO SOURCES OF MONETARY GROWTH

Conceivably we observe monetary growth to be associated with interest rates simply because it approximates, however imperfectly, the growth in credit. Interest rates depend upon the growth of credit insofar as the first-round effects of extending credit are important, and on growth of the total money stock insofar as money creation itself is important. A regression equation to test these effects is

$$i = \beta(dE) + \mu(dM - dE), \tag{1}$$

where i is the interest rate, E is net earning assets of the monetary system, M is the money stock as defined above, and d denotes changes in the variables. β and μ are coefficients: their value is a measure of the effect of monetary growth due to credit expansion (β) and all other sources (μ). Theoretically, β and μ may be zero or negative. If μ is zero, the residual sources have no effect on interest rates, and the entire effect of monetary growth can be attributed to credit effects. If both coefficients are negative and equal, the two sources of monetary growth have the same effect on interest rates. Credit expansion then plays no separate role, and the entire effect can be attributed to the portfolio effect as described in Chapter 1. For credit to have a separate additional effect, $\beta - \mu$ must be significantly negative.[2]

In the remainder of this chapter, estimates of these coefficients are presented.

___

[2] If $\beta - \mu$ were significantly *positive,* it would mean that monetary growth had less effect on interest rates when produced through credit expansion. This would not be consistent with either the credit or the portfolio theory.

PROBLEMS OF THE DATA

To estimate equation 1, the series on monetary growth used in the previous chapter were supplemented by data on the earning assets of the monetary system. Monthly Federal Reserve earning assets exclusive of loans to banks have been reported since 1914, and a monthly series for Treasury securities outstanding was also available. Asset data for all commercial banks, unfortunately, were not available on a monthly basis before World War II. There were data for all commercial banks annually since 1896 and monthly since 1948. The only earlier monthly data pertained to weekly reporting member banks since 1919. Reporting member banks have accounted for about half of total earning assets of all commercial banks.

Using reporting member banks to represent all commercial banks tends to reduce the size and significance of the coefficient of the credit variable. We may assess the size of the misrepresentation from Chart 4-3. The chart presents a scatter diagram of the stage-to-stage changes in credit growth, as used in the subsequent regressions, of all commercial banks and of reporting member banks for 1948–66, which the former data cover. The correlation coefficient is .92. It is high, both because reporting member banks are a good proxy for all commercial banks and because commercial banks contribute only one part of total credit along with the Federal Reserve and the Treasury. Since it exceeds the .42 correlation between credit and monetary growth for the same period (Chart 4-2), it suggests that the series for reporting member banks can be run with the money series to distinguish satisfactorily the effects on interest rates of credit and monetary growth. The statistical analysis therefore uses the reporting member bank data for the period since 1919. The errors due to misrepresentation are probably not negligible, however, so the series for all commercial banks, though available monthly only since 1948 and prior to that only annually, is also used in separate regressions as a check on the proxy series. Actually, the different data give similar results.

STATISTICAL RESULTS

Table 4-2 presents the three sets of regressions. To express the independent variables as growth rates, they have been divided by the

CHART 4-3

Growth in Net Earning Assets of the Consolidated Monetary System, Comparison Using Weekly Reporting Members and All Commercial Banks, Changes Between Reference Cycle Stages, 1948–66
(change in per cent per year)

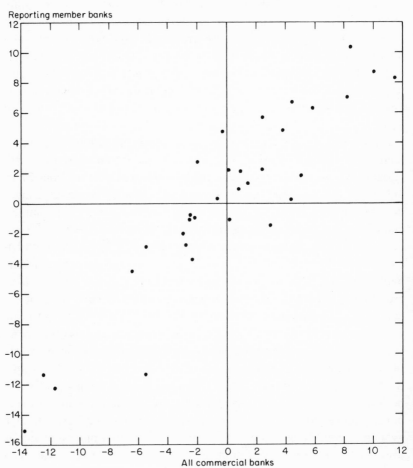

Source: Data appendix. For definition of variables, see Table 4-1.

money stock. Thus, equation 1 becomes

$$i = \beta(dE/M) + \mu[dM/M - dE/M].$$ (2)

The regressions of reference cycle stages exclude, as before, the war contractions and 1929–33, and the regressions of annual data also exclude all the war years 1940–46. The monetary and credit changes are so large during those years that their inclusion would dominate the annual regressions. The war years are unimportant in the reference stage regressions and need not be excluded, since they affect only part of one reference expansion. The regressions including dummy variables for cycle stages (as described in the appendix to Chapter 3) are discussed later.

All the regressions were made comparable to those in the previous chapter by taking *first differences* of equation 2 and adding a constant term not given in the table (see the note to Table 4-2). The dependent variable, therefore, is the stage-to-stage or annual change in the level of interest rates, and the independent variables are stage-to-stage changes in the average monthly rate of change (as in Chart 4-2) or year-to-year changes in the annual rate of change. The unit of measurement for the interest rates is the change per stage or per year in basis points (one hundredth of a percentage point); for the independent variables, it is the change per stage or per year in the monthly or annual rate of change, all expressed as the change in an annual percentage rate. A regression coefficient of -10, say, indicates that an increase of one percentage point in the annual growth rate would reduce interest rates by ten basis points.

In all the regressions the credit effect on interest rates (as indicated by the negative value of the difference between the coefficients) is generally from about 10 to 40 per cent of the effect of monetary growth given by μ. The only larger credit effects are shown by two of the regressions for corporate and municipal bonds and two for annual changes in government securities. But in general the differences are not statistically significant (their t values are nearly all less then 2.0).

The large credit coefficient for corporate and municipal bond yields in the 1948–66 period is anomalous and may be disregarded since its statistical significance is low. The relatively large credit coefficients for bill and bond yields in the annual changes, however, can be given

TABLE 4-2

Relation Between Interest Rates and Two Sources of Monetary Growth, Consolidated Monetary System Including Treasury, 1919–66 and 1948–66

Interest Rate and Period [a]	Partial Regression Coefficient [b]			Inclusion of Stage Dummy Variables	R
	Credit Expansion [c] (β)	Residual Monetary Growth (μ)	$(\beta - \mu)$ [d]		
	Changes Between Reference Cycle Stages				
1919–66					
Commercial paper	−5.2	−4.3(3.4)	−0.9(1.1)	NO	.43
	−5.0	−4.4(3.8)	−0.6(0.9)	YES	.67
Treasury bills	−6.2	−4.4(3.3)	−1.8(2.0)	NO	.49
	−6.3	−5.0(4.4)	−1.2(1.7)	YES	.75
U.S. bonds	−2.2	−2.1(4.0)	−0.1(0.3)	NO	.45
	−2.1	−2.1(3.7)	−0.0(0.1)	YES	.55
Corp. and municipal bonds	−2.9	−2.5(1.3)	−0.4(0.3)	NO	.17
	−1.7	−1.3(0.6)	−0.4(0.3)	YES	.34
1948–66					
Commercial paper	−12.7	−12.4(3.1)	−0.3(0.2)	NO	.55
	−6.7	−5.6(2.1)	−1.2(1.2)	YES	.90
Treasury bills	−13.7	−13.3(3.3)	−0.5(0.3)	NO	.58
	−8.2	−6.9(2.6)	−1.3(1.3)	YES	.91
U.S. bonds	−3.8	−3.7(2.5)	−0.1(0.2)	NO	.47
	−1.6	−1.2(1.3)	−0.4(1.2)	YES	.90
Corp. and municipal bonds	−12.1	−10.3(1.2)	−1.8(0.5)	NO	.28
	−4.8	−1.8(0.2)	−3.0(0.8)	YES	.56
	Annual Changes				
1919–66					
Commercial paper	−9.4	−7.9(3.0)	−1.5(0.6)	NO	.68
Treasury bills [e]	−11.5	−7.0(2.6)	−4.4(1.4)	NO	.60
U.S. bonds	−3.0	−0.6(0.5)	−2.4(2.2)	NO	.56
Corp. and municipal bonds	−2.7	−1.1(1.0)	−1.6(1.4)	NO	.52

Note: These regressions are first differences of equation 2 in the text:

$$\Delta i = \beta \Delta (dE/M) + \mu \Delta [(dM/M) - (dE/M)] + \text{constant}$$

(continued)

Notes to Table 4-2 (concluded)

where i is the interest rate; M, total money stock; and E, net earning assets of monetary system as defined in Table 4-1. E pertains to all commercial banks for reference stages 1948–61 and for annual changes, and to weekly reporting member banks for reference stages 1919–66. β and μ are regression coefficients. The operator Δ denotes first differences of reference-cycle stage average or of annual data.

For computation, all the regressions were run in the statistically equivalent form:

$$\Delta i = (\beta - \mu)\Delta(dE/M) + \mu\Delta(dM/M) + \text{constant}$$

in order to obtain the t value of the difference between the regression coefficients.

In the regressions so indicated, seven dummy variables were added, one for each stage-to-stage change but the last. For each stage change, the corresponding dummy variable was unity and the rest were zero. The regression coefficients of the dummy variables (not shown) are estimates of the average change in interest rates between each pair of stages relative to the average change for the omitted pair.

Source: See the data appendix.

[a] The 1919–66 regressions begin with the 1919 reference trough and end with an assumed business peak in December 1966, except for the Treasury bill series, which begins with the 1920 peak. Excluded stages are the same as for Table 3-1. The 1948–66 regressions begin with the 1948 reference peak, end with the 1966 peak, and have no intervening exclusions. The annual regressions cover the years indicated, excluding the ten annual changes 1929–33 and 1940–46.

[b] Units of regression coefficients are interest-rate change in basis points for increase in monetary growth rate of one percentage point per year (100 basis points equals 1 percentage point). Figures in parentheses are t values with signs omitted.

[c] t values were not computed for credit variable.

[d] Because of rounding, differences shown may not be the same as differences computed from the figures shown in the first two columns. Figures in parentheses are t values with signs omitted.

[e] Begins 1920.

a special explanation: They result from the inclusion of Treasury debt; when the Treasury debt is excluded, as is done later in Table 4-3, they fall more in line with the other regressions. Treasury debt issues can be expected to influence the government security market, and the effect may carry over to corporate and municipal bonds as well. The greater credit effect shows up mainly in the annual regressions, probably because the security market anticipates Treasury deficits ahead of time, and the annual observations cover a long enough time span to incorporate the anticipations of, as well as the actual, Treasury issues in one observation. The reference stages, on the other hand, are probably too short to incorporate both, if the anticipations tend to lead the actual Treasury issues by several months or more.

Explanations for some of the other differences between the three sets of regressions can also be suggested. First, the effect of both variables is generally weaker on bond yields, as was found in Chapter 3. This simply reflects the longer maturity of bonds and the smaller amplitude of fluctuation of their yields. Bond yields typically respond slowly to short-run influences. These results do not show, therefore, that monetary and credit effects have their first impact in the markets for short-term funds. This question is taken up in Chapter 5. Second, both regression coefficients are smaller (in absolute size) for the top set covering the full 1919–66 period, which suggests that the association between money and interest rates was weaker in the earlier period. Even so, $\beta - \mu$ is on the average about the same for 1948–66 as for 1919–66, implying that the weekly reporting member bank data used for the longer period are not seriously deficient for the purposes of these regressions. Third, both coefficients are larger (in absolute size) for the annual regressions than for the 1919–66 reference regressions, probably because the monetary effect on interest rates is distributed over time and the annual observations encompass more of it. This is supported by the time pattern of the effect, discussed in Chapter 7.

Aside from these minor differences, this evidence taken as a whole shows that new money affects interest rates no matter how it enters the economy, though it has an additional, marginal effect when it is created by an expansion of credit.

Common Cyclical Patterns

In the final stages of business upswings, when borrowers clamor for credit, banks may often be able, despite Federal Reserve efforts to restrain monetary growth, to expand total credit temporarily by reducing their reserve ratios; and, conversely, in business recessions, when loan demand contracts, banks may allow credit growth to taper off (total credit may even decline temporarily) by increasing their reserve ratios. This behavior over the business cycle might affect credit growth more than monetary growth. Demand deposits would increase commensurately with the credit expansion, but time deposits and currency might not. As a result of such shifts in the demand curve for loans along the supply curve of bank credit (for a given amount of reserves), the regression coefficient of the credit component, intended to show the negative slope of a given demand curve by means of shifts in supply, could be pulled toward zero and so be understated.

There is a simple test of this possibility. As a first approximation we may assume that shifts in the demand curve for bank loans occur in consonance with the stages of the business cycle, inasmuch as those shifts and business activity are usually highly correlated. We may then add dummy variables for the stage-to-stage changes, as described in the appendix to Chapter 3. Each stage change of the variables is thereby converted into a deviation from its average change in those stages. The partial regression coefficients for the independent variables in such regressions are largely independent of cyclical influences.

The estimates are presented in Table 4-2 along with the regressions already discussed. For the full period 1919–66, the dummy variables tend to reduce the credit effect relative to the portfolio effect and, for the 1948–66 period, to increase it. Although this may be no more than a statistical accident, it may reflect a difference in economic behavior. Monetary policy since World War II has produced greater inverse cyclical conformity in monetary growth than formerly, and interest rates have for a variety of reasons displayed greater conformity. As a result, the dummy variables in the later period may absorb relatively more of the common fluctuation between monetary growth and interest rates than between credit growth and interest rates.

Of course, by affecting the variables differently the dummy variables may produce misleading estimates. There is no easy way to tell which estimates are more reliable. We may best conclude that the true values probably lie somewhere between the two sets of estimates shown in Table 4-2. By either set the portfolio effect is clearly quite strong, while the credit component has an uncertain additional effect.

Exclusion of Treasury Debt Operations

As explained above, Treasury debt operations were consolidated with the banking system in Table 4-2 in order to cancel out transactions not involving the public, such as the sale of Treasury securities to the banking system. It is proper that such a transaction not affect the credit variable, because the transaction by itself does not affect total credit supplied to the public.

If banks reduce loans to the public to make room for the purchase of Treasury securities, that is equivalent for present purposes to a sale of Treasury securities to the public. In a sale to the public the credit variable is reduced. The logic of this procedure is that such a sale reduces the supply of credit — shifting the supply curve — available to private borrowers. This procedure implicitly assumes that Treasury debt operations reflect a shift in the supply curve rather than a movement along it. It assumes, in other words, that the operation affects interest rates but is not affected by them. The assumption may not be entirely valid since the supply of Treasury securities may partly depend inversely upon interest rates. To avoid the need to rely on this assumption in testing the credit theory, the regressions were rerun with Treasury debt operations excluded by following the alternative definition given in Table 4-1.

The results with the credit variable now covering just the Federal Reserve and commercial banks are about the same (Table 4-3). The residual monetary growth is somewhat less significant in most regressions here than in Table 4-2, and the credit effect is relatively larger, except for corporate and municipal bonds in the later period and, as noted earlier, for the annual regressions, though the differences are still not significant. The credit effect ranges up to one-half of the portfolio effect, and in one case — commercial paper 1948–66 — up to three-quarters.

The larger difference between these coefficients than between those in Table 4-2 could mean that it is inappropriate to include Treasury operations and that the true credit effect is indeed larger with the exclusion. On that interpretation Treasury debt operations are not entirely independent of interest rates and act as an extraneous element in the regressions. Yet, as noted, that is not true for the annual regressions. Furthermore, since the effect of excluding Treasury debt is greater for the 1948–66 period, another interpretation is more appealing. It is that Treasury debt, especially the short-term bills issued in such large volume after World War II, is a partial money substitute and should be added (presumably with a weight less than unity) to monetary liabilities rather than wholly deducted from earning assets of the monetary system. In that case, Treasury debt was inappropriately treated in Table 4-2, and its exclusion in Table 4-3 partially removed its biased effect on the credit variable, but also removed its effect from

A Test of the Credit and Portfolio Effects

75

TABLE 4-3

Relation Between Interest Rates and Two Sources of Monetary Growth, Consolidated Monetary System Excluding Treasury, 1919–66 and 1948–66

Interest Rate and Period	Partial Regression Coefficient			Inclusion of Stage Dummy Variables	R
	Credit Expansion (β)	Residual Monetary Growth (μ)	$\beta - \mu$		
Changes Between Reference Cycle Stages					
1919–66					
Commercial paper	−5.5	−3.8(2.8)	−1.7(1.4)	NO	.44
	−5.2	−4.1(3.2)	−1.2(1.0)	YES	.67
Treasury bills	−6.1	−4.2(2.9)	−1.8(1.4)	NO	.46
	−6.2	−4.8(3.8)	−1.4(1.2)	YES	.74
U.S. bonds	−2.5	−1.8(3.1)	−0.7(1.3)	NO	.47
	−2.4	−1.7(2.9)	−0.6(1.2)	YES	.56
Corp. and municipal bonds	−2.6	−2.8(1.3)	+0.2(0.1)	NO	.16
	−1.4	−1.6(0.7)	+0.1(0.1)	YES	.33
1948–66					
Commercial paper	−13.5	−10.0(2.5)	−3.5(1.4)	NO	.58
	−7.8	−4.6(1.8)	−3.3(1.9)	YES	.91
Treasury bills	−14.4	−11.4(2.8)	−3.1(1.2)	NO	.60
	−9.0	−7.0(2.6)	−2.0(1.1)	YES	.90
U.S. bonds	−3.9	−3.3(2.2)	−0.6(0.6)	NO	.48
	−1.7	−1.5(1.6)	−0.2(0.3)	YES	.89
Corp. and municipal bonds	−12.6	−10.9(1.2)	−1.7(0.3)	NO	.27
	−6.8	−1.8(0.2)	−5.0(0.7)	YES	.56
Annual Changes					
1919–66					
Commercial paper	−9.2	−7.8(2.6)	−1.4(0.5)	NO	.68
Treasury bills	−9.8	−7.8(2.4)	−2.0(0.7)	NO	.58
U.S. bonds	−2.6	−8.7(0.7)	−1.8(1.4)	NO	.52
Corp. and municipal bonds	−2.4	−1.6(1.2)	−0.8(0.7)	NO	.49

Source and notes: Same as for Table 4-2.

the money variable and thus reduced the measured monetary effect.

In either case, the main conclusion is unchanged: Money created by whatever means affects interest rates and the credit effect is only a fraction of the portfolio effect.

SEPARATION OF GOVERNMENT AND COMMERCIAL BANKS

In Chapter 2 it was argued that the beneficiaries of private money creation may strive to maintain some desired ratio of their imputed net worth to consumption. In doing so, they would largely offset additions to their imputed net worth due to credit expansion by banks and thus largely negate the effect of that expansion on the total supply of credit and thus on interest rates. This argument does not apply to government money creation, however. To whatever extent stockholders and depositors of commercial banks behave in that manner, taxpayers of the government would not necessarily behave similarly in response to government money creation. Government money created in lieu of debt issues has a much less certain effect on the discounted value of future taxes for debt servicing than money created by a commercial bank has on its net worth. It follows that money creation through credit expansion by the government may have a greater effect on interest rates than that of commercial banks. Combining the two sectors therefore dilutes the measured credit effect of the government.

In Table 4-4, this proposition is tested by dividing the credit variable into two components, one for commercial banks and one for the Federal Reserve. Loans to banks by the Federal Reserve now do not cancel, since there is no consolidation of the two sectors; these loans are treated as credit extended by the Federal Reserve and are deducted from the credit of commercial banks. Also, to avoid the possibility of underestimating the credit effect here, the Treasury is excluded. In terms of Table 4-1, commercial bank credit E_C is loans (line 14) plus investments (line 15) minus loans from Federal Reserve Banks (line 19). Federal Reserve credit E_F is earning assets (lines 2 + 3). The regression equation has three independent variables:

$$i = \beta_C(dE_C/M) + \beta_F(dE_F/M) + \mu[(dM - dE_C - dE_F)/M]. \qquad (3)$$

The proposition to be tested is whether $\beta_F - \beta_C$ is negative.

Generally, the proposition is supported by the test. With the inclusion of dummy variables, which, as explained above, tends to remove the response of bank credit to cycles in the private demand for credit, the effect of Federal Reserve credit is greater than the effect of commercial bank credit; and even without the dummy variables, Federal Reserve credit has the greater effect more often than not. (A puzzling exception is U.S. bond yields in the annual regressions. Perhaps this is an accident; I have no ready explanation.)

While consistent with the theory, this evidence is still no more than suggestive for two reasons. First, the differential effect of Federal Reserve credit is significantly greater by the t test in only two regressions, those with dummy variables for commercial paper and Treasury bill rates, 1919–66. And, second, when Treasury debt operations are consolidated with the Federal Reserve to form a variable of total government credit (not shown), these differences largely disappear.

CONCLUSIONS

The theories outlined in Chapter 1 imply that monetary growth affects interest rates inversely through portfolio adjustments and has an additional effect if created through credit expansion. In Chapter 2 it was argued that the credit effect is likely to be strongest for government money creation and to be temporary and uncertain for commercial bank money creation. In some monetary literature, on the other hand, the credit effect is viewed as the only or the main short-run monetary effect on interest rates.

This chapter presented a test of these propositions. Interest rates were regressed on two parts of monetary growth, one set representing credit expansion of commercial banks and the government, and a residual part representing all other sources of monetary growth. Credit was measured by growth in the earning assets of commercial banks, the Federal Reserve, and the Treasury. In some regressions all three were consolidated, in some just the former two with the Treasury excluded; and in some of these, commercial bank and Federal Reserve credit were treated as separate variables.

The results clearly indicated that monetary growth affects interest rates inversely no matter how it is created. If created through credit

TABLE 4-4

Relation Between Interest Rates and Three Sources of Monetary Growth, Consolidated Monetary System
Excluding Treasury, 1919–66 and 1948–66

Interest Rate and Period	Partial Regression Coefficient					Inclusion of Stage Dummy Variables	R
	Credit Expansion of		Residual Monetary Growth (μ)	$\beta_C - \mu$	$\beta_F - \mu$		
	Commercial Banks (β_C)	Federal Reserve (β_F)					
	Changes Between Reference Cycle Stages						
1919–66							
Commercial paper	−5.1	−7.9	−3.5(2.4)	−1.6(1.2)	−4.4(1.2)	NO	.45
	−3.8	−11.9	−3.0(2.3)	−0.9(0.8)	−8.9(2.5)	YES	.70
Treasury bills	−6.4	−5.1	−4.5(2.8)	−1.9(1.4)	−0.6(0.2)	NO	.47
	−5.2	−10.6	−4.0(3.0)	−1.1(1.0)	−6.6(1.9)	YES	.75
U.S. bonds	−2.5	−2.4	−1.8(3.0)	−0.7(1.3)	−0.6(0.4)	NO	.47
	−2.1	−3.8	−1.5(2.3)	−0.6(1.0)	−2.3(1.3)	YES	.57
Corp. and municipal bonds	−2.4	−3.7	−2.6(1.2)	+0.2(0.1)	−1.0(0.2)	NO	.17
	−0.2	−7.2	−0.7(0.3)	+0.4(0.2)	−6.5(1.0)	YES	.36

1948–66

Commercial paper	-13.7	-12.4	-10.2(2.4)	-3.6(1.4)	-2.2(0.4)	NO	.59
	-7.4	-9.5	-4.3(1.6)	-3.1(1.7)	-5.2(1.2)	YES	.91
Treasury bills	-9.7	-15.4	-12.1(2.9)	+2.4(0.4)	-3.3(1.3)	NO	.62
	-8.5	-10.6	-6.7(2.3)	-1.8(1.0)	-3.9(0.9)	YES	.91
U.S. bonds	-4.4	-1.5	-3.7(2.5)	-0.7(0.8)	+2.2(1.0)	NO	.54
	-1.6	-2.2	-1.5(1.4)	-0.2(0.2)	-0.7(0.4)	YES	.89
Corp. and municipal bonds	-13.0	-10.3	-11.2(1.2)	-1.8(0.3)	+0.9(0.1)	NO	.27
	-4.6	-7.5	-2.2(0.2)	-2.4(0.1)	-5.2(0.7)	YES	.56

Annual Changes

1919–66

Commercial paper	-8.9	-10.8	-7.9(2.6)	-1.0(0.3)	-2.9(0.4)	NO	.68
Treasury bills	-9.5	-12.5	-8.0(2.4)	-1.6(0.5)	-4.5(0.6)	NO	.58
U.S. bonds	-3.0	-0.9	-0.8(0.6)	-2.2(1.6)	-0.0(0.0)	NO	.52
Corp. and municipal bonds	-2.3	-3.0	-1.6(1.2)	-0.7(0.5)	-1.4(0.5)	NO	.49

Source and notes: Same as for Table 4-2, except for division of credit variable into two parts according to definition of Table 4-1.

expansion, however, the effect is greater generally by about 10 to 40 per cent, though several estimates fall beyond that range. But only a few of the credit coefficients are statistically significant. Federal Reserve credit treated separately apparently has a larger effect than commercial bank credit. While the magnitude of the credit effect is somewhat uncertain and marginal, the portfolio effect is strong and uniformly statistically significant.

These results pertain to the relative effects in the time span of the observations, that is from a few to many months for reference stages and to a year for the annual regressions. For shorter periods the credit effect may be relatively larger; for longer periods it is very likely even smaller.

Since bank credit is a sum of bank loans and investments, the effect of one of the components on interest rates may be even greater than the estimated effect of both together. This possibility is examined in Chapter 5.

5

The Components of
Bank Credit

The statistical analysis of the preceding chapter may underestimate the credit effect by not distinguishing between bank loans and investments, since they could influence particular interest rates differently. Bank loans, for example, should have the greatest impact on commercial paper and bank loan rates; and bank investments, on security yields. We can examine such differential effects by dividing the total earning assets of the banking system into loans to customers and purchases of securities on the open market. The latter consist of Federal Reserve credit outstanding exclusive of loans to member banks (item 2 in Table 4-1) plus investments of commercial banks (item 15). Mortgages are classified as loans in banking data, and only the annual data provide sufficient detail to treat them as investments, a more appropriate classification here because mortgage interest rates behave similarly to long-term rates.

Table 5-1 repeats the previous regressions, with the credit variable subdivided into loans, L, and investments, I (Treasury debt operations omitted). The regressions are in the form:

$$i = \beta_L \, dL + \beta_I dI + \mu(dM - dL - dI) \qquad (1)$$

where the third term on the right is the residual source of monetary growth excluding the contribution of bank credit. As before, the regressions were run as first differences, and in all of them the cyclical movement was held constant by dummy variables in order to remove the cyclical response of loans to credit demand. (Also, the figures in

The Channels of Monetary Effects on Interest Rates

TABLE 5-1

Relation Between Interest Rates and Two Components of Bank Credit, Consolidated Monetary System Excluding Treasury, 1919–61 and 1948–61

| | Partial Regression Coefficient | | | |
| | Expansion of | | | Residual Monetary Growth (μ) |
Interest Rate and Period	Loans (β_L)	Investments (β_I)	$\beta_L - \beta_I$	
	Changes Between Reference Cycle Stages			
1919–61				
Commercial paper	−3.1(3.2)	−3.1(3.8)	−0.1(0.0)	−2.6(3.4)
Bank loans	−2.2(3.9)	−1.1(2.2)	−1.1(1.9)	−1.1(2.4)
Treasury bills	−2.9(2.9)	−4.0(4.9)	+1.0(0.9)	−3.3(4.1)
U.S. bonds	−1.4(2.9)	−1.5(3.7)	+0.1(0.2)	−1.1(2.9)
Corp. and municipal bonds	−1.4(3.0)	−0.9(2.2)	−0.5(1.1)	−1.1(2.8)
1948–61				
Commercial paper	−7.7(2.1)	−6.1(3.0)	−1.7(0.5)	−4.5(2.1)
Bank loans	−2.4(1.5)	−1.4(1.6)	−1.0(0.8)	−1.1(1.2)
Treasury bills	−6.2(1.4)	−8.0(3.3)	+1.8(0.5)	−6.7(2.6)
U.S. bonds	−1.3(0.9)	−1.4(1.8)	+0.1(0.1)	−1.2(1.4)
Corp. and municipal bonds	−3.8(1.9)	−1.9(1.7)	+2.0(1.2)	−1.7(1.5)
	Annual Changes			
Commercial paper, 1896–1963	−9.5(6.4)	−6.5(4.9)	−3.0(1.7)	−7.5(3.6)
Treasury bills, 1920–63	−5.5(1.8)	−4.4(2.6)	−1.1(0.4)	−5.4(2.1)
U.S. bonds, 1919–62	−2.8(3.1)	−1.3(1.9)	−1.5(1.7)	−1.2(1.0)
Corp. and municipal bonds, 1900–63	−2.4(3.9)	−1.1(2.2)	−1.3(1.8)	−1.5(1.8)

Note: Figures in parentheses are t values with signs omitted. These regressions are based on equation 1 in the text.

Changes between reference stage averages:

$$\Delta i = \beta_L \Delta[dL/(L+I)] + \beta_I \Delta[dI/(L+I)] + \mu \Delta\{[dM/(L+I)]$$
$$- [d(L+I)/(L+I)]\} + \Sigma_1^7 \delta_s D_s + \text{constant}.$$

(continued)

Notes to Table 5-1 (concluded)

Changes between annual rates of change:

$$\Delta i = \beta_L \Delta(dL/M) + \beta_I \Delta(dI/M) + \mu \Delta\{(dM/M) - [d(L + I)/M]\} + \delta D + \text{constant}$$

where i is the interest rate; M, total money stock; L loans of commercial banks; and I Federal Reserve credit outstanding exclusive of loans to banks plus investments of commercial banks. The D's are dummy variables, as explained in the appendix to Chapter 3. β_L, β_I, μ, and δ are regression coefficients. The operator Δ denotes first differences in reference stage averages or in annual data. For 1919–61, L and I pertain to weekly reporting member banks; for 1948–61, to all commercial banks. For reference stage averages based on monthly data, mortgages are classified in the original data as loans, but for annual changes as investments (correctly for present purposes).

Unlike the regressions in the previous chapter, the independent variables for reference stages here were divided by earning assets rather than the money stock. In the reference stage equations, $dL/d(L + I)$, $dI/d(L + I)$, and $dM/d(L + I)$ are reference stage averages of monthly percentage changes, converted to annual rates. However, $dM/d(L + I)$ was approximated by $(dM/M) \cdot [M/(L + I)]$, in which reference stage averages were computed *before* taking the product, because stage averages of dM/M were already available.

Source: See the data appendix.

Table 5-1 were computed at an earlier time than those in the foregoing tables. As explained in the note to Table 5-1, these regressions were run with slightly different versions of some of the variables and have earlier terminal dates; two of the annual regressions have an earlier starting date. But these differences are minor.)

The credit theory implies that the loan coefficient should be larger in absolute value than the investment coefficient for commercial paper and bank loan rates, and smaller for security yields. The results only faintly support that implication. For commercial paper and bank loan rates, the absolute value of the regression coefficient for loans is indeed slightly larger than that for investments, and vice versa for Treasury bill and U.S. bond yields, except in the annual regressions. For the other bond series and the annual regressions, however, the coefficients are not uniformly consistent with the credit theory. In particular, the effect of investments is not generally greater on security yields than the effect of loans. Moreover, no pair of loan and investment coefficients differs significantly at the .05 level, though that for bank loans 1919–61 almost does.

Furthermore, if we compare the two credit effects with that of residual monetary growth, the former are not relatively larger (in absolute value) here than they were in Chapter 4, where loans and investments were not separated. Failure to make the separation, therefore, does not produce an underestimate of the credit effect.

If there were little or no arbitrage among financial markets, credit expansion in particular markets would affect local interest rates. The results suggest some initial effect, but it is slight and apparently short-lived, even for the markets for which bank credit supposedly plays a dominant role — commercial paper and bank loans.

The cornerstone of the credit theory is the alleged independence of financial markets. Special circumstances may produce partial independence, as in the mortgage market. But, in general, studies which have looked for individual supply effects in particular financial markets have found the effects to be weak or nonexistent. Alternative opportunities for demanders and access by alternative suppliers appear to keep these subsectors in line with the financial market as a whole. The present results confirm this conclusion.

6

A Model of Monetary
Effects on Interest Rates

This chapter presents a model of the portfolio effect described in Chapter 1. The purpose is to explain the empirical results of Chapters 4 and 5 and to show how variations in monetary growth that are not due to bank lending can still affect interest rates. New money is channeled into financial markets, not only initially when lent by banks but also subsequently by the recipients of the additional money as it circulates through the economy. The model gives results broadly consistent with the evidence.

FORMULATION OF THE MODEL

The following assumptions of the model fall within the usual simplifications found in the literature. The first-round effects of money creation are ignored, so that the means of issue need not be specified. In addition to money there is one uniform security which is the vehicle for all borrowing and lending in the economy. To simplify matters further, it is assumed that all investment expenditures are financed by current borrowing (selling new securities) and encompass the total demand for credit or loanable funds. The total supply comprises lending by households, which is derived from two sources: from saving part of current income to add to wealth and from transferring money into securities to change the form in which wealth already accumulated is held. The reverse transfer—from securities into money—reduces the supply of credit or loanable funds.[1]

Such portfolio transfers are induced by the emergence of a discrepancy between desired and actual holdings of securities and money in the sense that current holdings do not correspond with the long-run desired disposition of wealth. People are willing to hold undesired amounts in the short run until at their convenience they make adjustments. Emphasis on such discrepancies as the origin of monetary effects on interest rates in this dynamic model is the point of departure from the usual static analysis.

Portfolio transfers of money represent a flow supply of funds. In the model the net flow is made proportional—as a plausible first approximation—to the percentage discrepancy between actual and desired holdings,

$$c \ln (M^s/M^d) \tag{1}$$

where M^s is actual money balances (the outstanding stock) and M^d the desired level. The constant positive parameter c indicates the size of the resulting transfer; it converts a percentage discrepancy into the units of a rate of change of expenditure. If c equaled, say, 0.5 per year, an excess of actual over desired balances of 10 per cent would produce transfers at the rate of 5 per cent per year. If, instead, people acted on the average to remove a discrepancy entirely within, say, three months, c would be 4 per year. (The time dimension of c has to be the same as that for expenditures in the model.)

In the monetary literature the two principal variables found to affect desired money balances are nominal income (Y) and interest rates, represented here by i, the market rate on the one uniform security. Aggregate expenditure and income are assumed to be identical. The re-

---

[1] Some transactions cut across this subdivision and must be classified arbitrarily. Borrowing to increase money holdings does not add to investment expenditures and so may be treated as a deduction from the supply of loanable funds; it should be netted against transfers from money to securities. Saving to increase money holdings does not add to the supply of loanable funds but is canceled by an implicit transfer from securities to money. Investment financed by selling old securities from portfolio is equivalent to a transfer of wealth from securities to money combined with borrowing from oneself; the source of the funds is a reduction in someone's desired money balances. By such interpretations of the definitions of borrowing, saving, and transfers, the assumption that investment expenditures equal total current borrowing can be preserved.

lation may be written

$$\ln M^d = \ln Y - bi, \qquad (2)$$

where the income elasticity of demand is, for simplicity, assumed to be unity.[2] The constant parameter b is positive. A rise in the interest rate reduces desired balances according to the demand function for money balances. The use of current income rather than permanent income or wealth in the equation is a departure from the practice of the latest empirical studies. (The use of permanent income is discussed in the appendix to this chapter.) The rate of change of prices, which appears to affect desired money balances importantly only in times of very rapid inflation, is also ignored.

How a discrepancy between actual and desired balances arises and how it affects the interest rate is best described by an example.

Suppose there is a change in M^s starting from a position of equilibrium in which actual and desired balances are equal. Figure 6-1 shows M^d in relation to i for a given Y, the initial interest rate i_q for M_0^s and the new stock M_1^s. The increase in the money stock to M_1^s would, if the rate fell to i_1, make $M^s = M^d$. But the attempts of money holders to exchange their excess balances for securities will not produce a rate as low as i_1. The rate declines as moneyholders bid for securities, but with the result that investment (borrowing) demand increases and saving (lending) declines, which thus raises the supply of securities and reduces the demand. Equilibrium in the loan market requires, for the moment, some intermediate rate i_2 between i_q and i_1 which equates the *total* demand and supply of securities. The flow of funds supplied out of the discrepancy between actual and desired money balances is part of the demand for securities. It makes up the difference between investment and saving $(I - S)$. The size of the discrepancy at any time therefore helps determine the values of the two variables in the system, i and Y. We may consider the determination of each in turn.

[2] A parameter other than unity could be inserted without difficulty as a factor in the first term. So long as this parameter is unity, the logarithm of the price index can be subtracted from both sides of the equation to put the money stock and income in real terms, a more conventional form of the demand equation. This change makes no essential difference, and for convenience it has not been done here.

If the coefficient of the income term is not unity, however, the adjustment to real terms does make a difference and must be done explicitly.

FIGURE 6-1

Effect of Desired and Actual Balances on Interest Rate

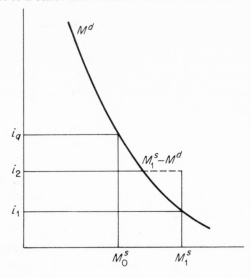

The Determination of i

Investment and saving are functions of income and the interest rate. If the functions are linear and invariant to growth in dollar amounts, we may write

$$(I - S)/Y = -n(i - i_q) \qquad (3)$$

where i_q is the equilibrium rate and n is a positive constant. A difference between investment and saving as a percentage of income is produced at any given interest rate by a flow of funds originating in the discrepancy between actual and desired balances. Then, from (1),

$$i - i_q = -a \ln (M^s/M^d) \qquad (4)$$

determines the interest rate, where $a = c/n$. Equation 4 is the heart of the model and is a simple way to rationalize the empirical results presented above.

As noted above, the model disregards any first-round effect of issuing money. Such effects involve a change in the saving of the issuers of money and could be introduced by adding, for example, some fraction of the growth in the money stock to the supply of loanable funds. The model also makes no allowance for the effect of changing prices on nominal interest rates: an expansion of the money supply increases prices and eventually the expectation of price changes, which tends to *raise* nominal interest rates and to counteract the effect of changing prices on the value of fixed-dollar securities. This effect of inflation on nominal interest rates is ignored here.

Equation 4 could be written, instead, as

$$\frac{di}{dt} = -a \ln (M^s/M^d) \qquad (4')$$

if it is reasoned that the interest rate would change until the discrepancy was erased. But $(4')$ ignores the effect of the interest rate on investment and saving and their role in the loanable funds market, since the equation says that the interest rate keeps changing so long as actual and desired money balances are unequal. Certain day-to-day adjustments in portfolios may be explained by equation $4'$, but it is inappropriate to the intermediate-run movements examined in this study. Moreover, equation $4'$ leads to a relation between the level of the interest rate and of current and past *stocks* of money, whereas the model is designed to explain a dependence of the level of the interest rate on the current and past *rates of change* of the money stock.[3]

The Determination of Y [4]

An excess of investment over saving is financed by the lending of undesired money holdings. The increased flow of lending supplied by the discrepancy raises investment expenditures and produces a rising level of income. The growth of income continues so long as the discrepancy does. Income also grows, even if the discrepancy is zero, by the expected trend of income, which is anticipated and allowed for ahead of time. The expected growth of income equals the average rate of growth of real income (g_0, assumed constant) plus the expected rate of change of prices, $d \ln P^e/dt$. If current income moves along the expected trend, the variables maintain an equilibrium relationship; in particular, de-

---

[3] For an analysis of the kind implied by equation $4'$ see William E. Gibson, "Interest Rates and Monetary Policy," *Journal of Political Economy,* May/June 1970.

[4] It is necessary to specify how Y is determined in the model, because Y affects M^d.

sired and actual money balances grow at the trend rate and remain equal. Income growth departs from the expected trend when actual and desired balances diverge.

The equation for income growth can be written

$$\frac{d \ln Y}{dt} = c \ln (M^s/M^d) + \frac{d \ln P^e}{dt} + g_0. \tag{5}$$

The use of the same coefficient c here as in (1) implies that all adjustments of money balances involve the purchase and sale of securities. This is not necessary, however, and the discrepancy in (5) can be interpreted as including some expenditures directly on goods and services as well as some indirectly on capital goods through the net purchase of new securities.

Undesired money balances lead to increases in income, which in turn tend to remove the discrepancy by raising M^d. Hence the equality between the total demand and supply of loanable funds implied by (4) describes a moving equilibrium which determines i at each moment in time; it is continually changing to produce new values of i and Y. Equations 4 and 5 can be regarded as a simple extension of the usual static equilibrium analysis. In the static analysis with full employment and flexible prices, monetary growth raises nominal income and prices without affecting the equilibrium interest rate, which remains at i_q. The present model describes the path to that equilibrium when the system is disturbed. The use here of liquidity preference and loanable funds is quite conventional; together the two provide a stock-flow analysis of the movement to equilibrium.[5] All that has been added here is the idea of a temporary discrepancy between desired and actual balances which allows a simplified description of the movement in terms of a differential equation.

This formulation eliminates the crucial importance of the money demand function which it has in static models. In equation 2, b could be quite small with no important alteration in behavior of the variables. Presumably b would not be zero, for that would imply that money balances and securities are not substitutes in portfolios. The only consequence of a large b is that the full effect on income of an increase

---

[5] Credit for first combining liquidity preference and loanable funds in a stock-flow analysis of monetary changes belongs to George Horwich, *Money, Capital, and Prices*, Homewood, Ill., R. D. Irwin, 1964 (see also his earlier work cited therein).

in monetary growth is quite prolonged. The lending of excess balances reduces interest rates, which raises the desired balances. The desired increase in balances absorbs part of the excess, to that extent temporarily closing part of the discrepancy in money balances and delaying the full rise in expenditures and income. In the new long-run equilibrium the full effect on income of an increase in monetary growth is the same as it would be if desired balances did not depend upon interest rates.

To complete the model we need to specify how price expectations are formed. They are assumed to depend upon the discrepancy between actual and expected price changes; such a relation is commonly used in economic models. Since the adjustment is by all indications slow, we may simplify the mathematics by using the trend of the actual price change, $(d \ln P/dt)_q$, rather than the concurrent change, as follows:

$$\frac{d^2 \ln P^e}{dt^2} = f\left[\left(\frac{d \ln P}{dt}\right)_q - \frac{d \ln P^e}{dt}\right] \tag{6}$$

where the constant parameter f is positive. The trend of price changes can be approximated by the average rate of monetary growth less the average rate of growth in real income,

$$\left(\frac{d \ln P}{dt}\right)_q = \left(\frac{d \ln M^s}{dt}\right)_q - g_0. \tag{7}$$

We may also specify that $(d \ln M^s/dt)_q$ is an exponentially weighted average (with slope h) of the actual past rates of monetary growth. The approximation (7) will be reasonably accurate and consistent with the other equations in the model, provided that no major long-run changes in M^d occur due to changes in i. This supposition is plausible, since changes in i in this model are small and temporary, and the value of b is relatively low (about 0.5, according to most studies).

If we treat the money stock as exogenous, the above equations form a complete system and can be combined to eliminate all but one endogenous variable. The reduced form is a second-order differential equation. To derive it in terms of the interest rate, we differentiate (5) with respect to time and eliminate the price variables by successive substitution of (6), (7), and (5). Income, desired money balances, and their derivatives can be eliminated by means of (2), (4), and their derivatives.

(Also, $d^2 \ln M^s / dt^2$ is assumed to be zero, because only discrete changes in monetary growth will be analyzed.) The final result is

$$[(1/a) + b](d^2i/dt^2) + \{[(c + f)/a] - bf\}(di/dt) + (cf/a)i$$
$$= (cf/a)i_q + f[(d \ln M^s/dt)_q - (d \ln M^s/dt)]. \quad (8)$$

SOLUTION OF THE MODEL

To solve the differential equation 8 for i we must specify the time path of monetary growth. We may illustrate the behavior of the model by analyzing the simple case in which the money stock has grown at the constant rate g_0 up to time zero and then begins to grow at the higher constant rate g_1. Up to $t = 0$, i will have been constant at i_q.

By the definition of $(d \ln M^s/dt)_q$ we have, for $t \geqslant 0$,

$$\left(\frac{d \ln M^s}{dt}\right)_q - \frac{d \ln M^s}{dt} = h \int_{-\infty}^{0} g_0 e^{h(T-t)} \, dT + h \int_{0}^{t} g_1 e^{h(T-t)} \, dT - g_1$$
$$= -(g_1 - g_0)e^{h(T-t)} \quad (9)$$

where $he^{h(T-t)}$ is the weighting pattern (which sums to unity when T goes from $-\infty$ to t). Consequently, a particular solution of (8) is simply

$$i_t = i_q - J(g_1 - g_0)e^{-ht} \quad (10)$$

where J is a constant, and substitution of (10) in (8) shows that [6]

$$J = \frac{-af}{(h - f)[c - h(1 + ab)]}. \quad (11)$$

In the long run, therefore, i will approach i_q; there is no permanent effect of monetary growth on the interest rate (ignoring as we do any changes in the marginal productivity of capital i_q).

A general solution is given by the homogeneous equation, setting the right side of (8) equal to zero. Its discriminant [7] is

$$\left(\frac{c + f}{a} + bf\right)^2 - 4\left(\frac{1}{a} + b\right)\frac{cf}{a} = \left[\frac{c - f(1 + ab)}{a}\right]^2. \quad (12)$$

The quadratic equation associated with the homogeneous equation, therefore, has the roots

[6] My thanks to Carl Christ for pointing out an algebraic error at this point in an earlier version of this chapter.

[7] A homogeneous second-order differential equation with constant coefficients may be represented by $p(d^2i/dt^2) + q(di/dt) + ri = 0$. Its discriminant is $q^2 - 4pr$.

$$\frac{\dfrac{c+f}{a} + bf \pm \left(\dfrac{c - f(1 + ab)}{a}\right)}{2\left(\dfrac{1}{a} + b\right)} = -f \text{ and } \frac{-c}{1 + ab}. \qquad (13)$$

The complete general solution of (8) is the sum of (10) and two exponential terms with powers given by (13), that is,

$$i_t = i_q - J(g_1 - g_0)e^{-ht} + Ke^{-ft} + Le^{-[c/(1+ab)]t} \qquad (14)$$

where K and L are arbitrary constants of integration.

K and L are limited by certain specified conditions of the solution. Before $t = 0$, $i = i_q$; hence, K and L contain the factor $(d \ln M^s/dt) - g_0$ which is zero up to $t = 0$ and equals $g_1 - g_0$ thereafter. At the moment $t = 0$ when monetary growth jumps to g_1, no discrepancy in money balances has had time to develop and i still equals i_q. Hence $i_0 = i_q$ and

$$K + L = J(g_1 - g_0). \qquad (15)$$

Further restrictions on K and L can be derived from the specification that i initially declines after monetary growth increases. It is also necessary, however, to rank the exponents by size. From the derivation of the model it seems likely that $c/(1 + ab)$ is considerably larger than h, and the latter somewhat larger than f. It then follows that J as given by (11) and K are negative.[8] L may be positive or negative by these initial conditions, but it is most likely positive.[9]

[8] That K is negative follows from the assumption that $(di/dt)_0$ is negative. To show this, first differentiate (14) and set $t = 0$; then

$$(di/dt)_0 = -fK - [c/(1 + ab)]L + hJ(g_1 - g_0) < 0. \qquad (16)$$

Since K and L contain the factor $(g_1 - g_0)$, define $K' = K/(g_1 - g_0)$ and $L' = L/(g_1 - g_0)$, where K' and K have the same sign and likewise L' and L. Hence, from (15), $K' + L' = J$. We can then write (16) as

$$K'(h - f) - L'\{[c/(1 + ab)] - h\} < 0. \qquad (17)$$

If K' were positive, L' would also have to be positive. But that is impossible, since $K' + L' = J$ is negative. Hence K' and K are negative.

[9] L and L' can be positive or negative. If negative, however, L' must be appreciably smaller in absolute value than K', because of (17) and the assumption that $[c/(1 + ab)] - h$ greatly exceeds $h - f$. But the closer L' is to zero, the more the long-run influences in the model dominate the initial short-run movements (that is, the third term of (14) becomes unimportant). If the model is at all relevant to monetary effects on interest rates, the third term of (14) will be important, which requires that L' be positive and relatively large. The figure has been drawn accordingly. If $(di/dt)_0 = 0$, it can be shown that L is negative, but there is no reason to impose such a condition.

The solution is illustrated by Figure 6-2, assuming L is positive and K is negative but that otherwise their values are arbitrary. The interest rate first declines, then gradually returns to its original level.[10]

A once-and-for-all change in the money stock can be analyzed as a rise in the monetary growth rate which terminates after a short period of time. The solution can be found in the same manner by taking account of the two steps—first up, then down—in the monetary growth rate,[11] as in Figure 6-3. After first declining, the interest rate gradually returns to its original position, but more rapidly, of course, than for a continuing rise in monetary growth. In Figure 6-3, where the parameters have the same values as in Figure 6-2 and the constants of integration the same initial values, there is a slight temporary overshooting of the long-run equilibrium position. (Not all possible values of the constants produce overshooting.)

DESCRIPTION OF THE SOLUTION

Certain characteristics of the solution deserve attention. With an unanticipated increase in monetary growth, actual balances begin to grow faster than the desired amount. The public responds by increasing the flow of spending and lending. The lending reduces interest rates

[10] This can be shown by examining the number of times that di/dt becomes zero. We have

$$di/dt = -fKe^{-ft} - [c/(1 + ab)]Le^{-[c/(1+ab)]t} + hJ(g_1 - g_0)e^{-ht} = 0. \qquad (18)$$

Since $K' + L' = J$, equation (18) gives

$$K'(-fe^{-ft} + he^{-ht}) = L'\{[c/(1 + ab)]e^{-[c/(1+ab)]t} - he^{-ht}\}. \qquad (19)$$

The functions on each side of (19) have the same general pattern as that for i in Figure 6-2: starting above zero, they decline below zero, reach a mimimum point, and then approach zero asymptotically from below. If L' is positive (and K' negative), the left-hand side is inverted and forms a hill, while the right-hand side forms a valley, and the two then intersect only once; after the first intersection, the right-hand function remains below the left-hand function and approaches the zero line from below. That means there is only one value of t which satisfies (18) and (19).

[11] If monetary growth jumps from a rate of g_0 to g_1 during the interval from 0 to θ and then drops back to g_0, we have, instead of (9), for $t \geq \theta$

$$(d \ln M^s/dt)_q - (d \ln M^s/dt) = (g_1 - g_0)(e^{h\theta} - 1)e^{-ht}.$$

The values of K and L for $t \geq \theta$ can then be found by the condition that i_θ has the same value by the new and the old constants. These values are given in the note to Figure 6-3, where $\theta = .5$.

FIGURE 6-2

Graphical Solution of Equation 14 with Increase in Monetary Growth Rate

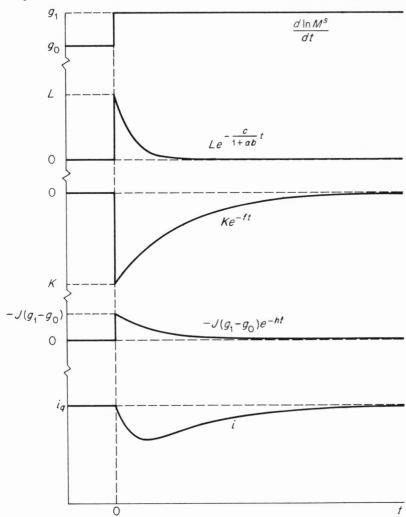

(described by equation 4) and, along with the greater spending (described by equation 5), increases the growth of income and the rate of change of prices. The increase in income growth and fall in interest rates raise the growth rate of desired balances, but not enough at first to prevent the discrepancy between actual and desired money balances

FIGURE 6-3

Graphical Solution of Equation 14 for Temporary Spurt
in Monetary Growth Rate

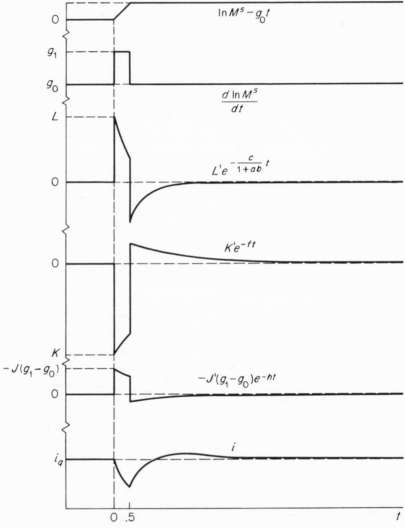

Note: For $t < 0.5$, $L' = L$, $K' = K$, $J' = J$. For $t \geq 0.5$, $L' = -L(e^{0.5c/(1+ab)} - 1)$, $K' = -K(e^{0.5f} - 1)$, $J' = -J(e^{0.5h} - 1)$.

from enlarging. Eventually the increase in income growth raises the growth rate of desired balances sufficiently to begin to reduce the discrepancy, and interest rates slowly return to initial levels. (The model disregards the possibility that interest may remain forever lower because of a fall in the marginal productivity of capital resulting from the increase in the capital stock.)

In long-run equilibrium, desired money balances rise at the new rate of monetary growth; the growth in nominal income due to price increases keeps money demand growing at that rate, and no new discrepancy occurs so long as the growth of the money stock remains constant at the new rate.

The path for the growth rate of nominal income will necessarily involve some overshooting. The effect of a sudden increase in monetary growth is to reduce the ratio M^s/Y, whereas in the final equilibrium this ratio returns to its original level.[12] Hence the cumulative percentage changes in money and income are equal. If the percentage change in income is initially below that of the money stock, therefore, the former must for a time exceed the latter.

If desired money balances depend upon permanent rather than current income, there is an additional reason for overshooting of income growth,[13] as shown in the appendix to this chapter.

APPENDIX: MODIFICATION OF THE MODEL USING PERMANENT INCOME

The model of Chapter 6 departs, as noted above, from the practice of empirical studies that use permanent income in the demand-for-money equation. With this modification the basic equations of the model are

[12] The final equilibrium will be different if the income elasticity of the demand for real money balances is not unity and if part of a change in money income is in real terms.

[13] On this point see also A. A. Walters, "Professor Friedman and the Demand for Money" and "The Demand for Money—The Dynamic Properties of the Multiplier," *Journal of Political Economy,* October 1965, pp. 545–51 and June 1967, pp. 293–98, respectively. Walters shows that a dependence of money demand on permanent income produces an overshooting in the adjustment of current income to monetary changes. But his analysis does not allow for a discrepancy between desired and actual balances and so does not have a lag in the initial effect on income of a monetary change, as does the model here.

$$\ln M^d = \ln Y_p - bi \tag{1A}$$

$$\frac{d \ln Y}{dt} = c(\ln M^s - \ln M^d) + \frac{d \ln P^e}{dt} + g_0 \tag{2A}$$

$$i - i_q = -a(\ln M^s - \ln M^d) \tag{3A}$$

$$\frac{d^2 \ln P^e}{dt^2} = f\left[\left(\frac{d \ln P}{dt}\right)_q - \frac{d \ln P^e}{dt}\right] \tag{4A}$$

where Y_p is permanent income. It may be formed by the usual adaptive adjustment as follows: [14]

$$\frac{d \ln Y_p}{dt} = p(\ln Y - \ln Y_p) + \frac{d \ln P^e}{dt} + g_0. \tag{5A}$$

The last two terms of (5A) impart the expected trend to permanent income, which then grows at the trend rate when there is no discrepancy between the actual and the permanent level.

The reduced form of these equations, containing the interest rate, the money stock, and their derivatives, is a third-order differential equation with an overabundance of possible solutions. The model can be simplified by dropping the expected-price-change variable and equation 4A, which determines it, on the assumption that the adjustment of this variable to the current change is slow (f is presumably very small) and that therefore its effects on short-run movements in the interest rate and income are only slight. (Its effect on M^d is ignored here.) The simpler model has an analytic solution and may be legitimately used for an analysis of once-and-for-all monetary changes which do not affect the long-run trend.

With the expected price change omitted, the model is reduced by differentiating (5A) with respect to time, substituting for the derivatives of Y_p and Y by means of (1A) and (2A), and removing the derivatives of M^d by means of (3A). The resulting equation can be written

$$\left(\frac{1}{a} + b\right)\frac{d^2 i}{dt^2} + \left(\frac{p}{a} + pb\right)\frac{di}{dt} + \left(\frac{pc}{a}\right)i = \left(\frac{pc}{a}\right)i_q + p\left(g_0 - \frac{d \ln M^s}{dt}\right). \tag{6A}$$

This equation has a general solution, given a specified change in monetary growth. Suppose that the monetary growth rate rises from

[14] See Milton Friedman, *A Theory of the Consumption Function,* Princeton for NBER, 1957, p. 143.

g_0 to g_1 at $t = 0$ and after one period drops back to g_0 and remains at that rate. A particular solution of (6A) then is

$$i = i_q - (a/c)(g_1 - g_0) \text{ for } 0 \leqslant t < 1$$
$$i = i_q \qquad\qquad\qquad \text{for } t \geqslant 1. \tag{7A}$$

The solution of the homogeneous equation is the sum of two exponential terms with powers given by the roots of the quadratic equation formed from the coefficients on the left side of (6A):

$$[(1/a) + b]X^2 + [(p/a) + pb]X + (pc/a) = 0.$$

The roots are

$$X = \frac{-p \pm \{ p^2 - [4pc/(1 + ab)]\}^{1/2}}{2}. \tag{8A}$$

The expression inside the braces can be written

$$[p/(1 + ab)][p(1 + ab) - 4c]. \tag{9A}$$

This quantity is negative on assumptions like those made in Chapter 6 that c exceeds the coefficient of expectation (here p) and that $1 + ab$ is well below 4. Consequently, the roots are complex and the general solution of (6A) may be written

$$i_t = e^{-pt/2}(A \sin \eta t + B \cos \eta t) + i_q \tag{10A}$$

where $t \geqslant 1$, η is the square root of the negative of (9A) and is therefore a positive real number, and A and B are constants of integration determined by initial conditions.

The effect on the interest rate of a change in the money stock therefore involves damped oscillations, with overshooting of the long-run equilibrium position. The reason for this result is not hard to see in terms of the modified model. The adjustment to an emerging discrepancy between actual and desired money balances is delayed by the lagged response of permanent income to changes in current income. Consequently, current income grows and interest rates decline more than would otherwise be necessary, and the delayed adjustments to these changes then push the variables too far in the opposite direction. As a result, the variables continually overshoot the equilibrium position (though by less and less).

7

The Lag in Monetary Effects
on Interest Rates and
Aggregate Expenditures

The theory of monetary effects on interest rates developed in the preceding chapter implies a particular pattern for those effects. With an increase in the rate of monetary growth, interest rates first decline and subsequently move back toward their initial level. In the particular model displayed there, the effect on real rates of interest is not permanent, and they eventually return to their starting point, though overshooting and oscillations may occur on the path to the final equilibrium. In addition, the Fisher effect of anticipated inflation on nominal interest rates increases them further, though the complete effect may take a long time.

In this chapter, the lag pattern is examined statistically for its conformity to the theory. In the second part of the chapter these results are compared with the related lag of monetary effects on aggregate expenditures.

THE LAGGED EFFECT ON
INTEREST RATES

The statistical analysis presented here does not impose any particular shape beforehand on the time pattern of the lag, but for simplicity we assume that it remains the same. This requires that the regression observations be dated at equal intervals. The reference-stage averages used in previous chapters vary in duration of coverage and would be applicable here if the lag time at each point varied in proportion to the duration of the concomitant reference phase. Instead, fixed, rather than variable, lags are used here.

The regressions are of the form

$$\Delta i_t = \alpha + \beta_1 \Delta m_t + \beta_2 \Delta m_{t-1} + \beta_3 \Delta m_{t-2} + \cdots + \beta_{n+1} \Delta m_{t-n},$$

where i is the interest rate, m_t is the monetary growth rate in month or quarter t (adjusted to include deposits of unlicensed banks March 1933 to June 1935), α and β are regression coefficients, and the operator Δ indicates the first differences of the variables. The equation relates the change in the interest rate during period t to changes in monetary growth rates in t and previous periods back to $t - n$. A permanent change in the monetary growth rate affects the interest rate by β_1 in the first period, by β_2 in the second period, and so on. The sum of the coefficients gives the total effect of an increase in the monetary growth rate which starts in period $t - n$ and remains at the augmented rate for the subsequent n periods.

First differences are used to abstract from long-run influences on interest rates. Taking first differences does not affect the economic interpretation of the coefficients except for the constant term.

Chart 7-1 presents the cumulative lag pattern of the commercial paper rate for the period 1910–65 and for two subperiods. These patterns are based on regressions of monthly data, which for the money stock begin in the middle of 1907. The first observation of the independent variable included in the regressions is the change in the monetary growth rate from June to July 1907, and the first observation included of the interest rate is the change from August to September 1910, thirty-nine months later. Monetary growth is expressed as an annual percentage rate.

The chart should be interpreted as follows: Suppose the annual rate of monetary growth increases by one percentage point. At first the interest rate declines and later begins to rise. For the regression of the full period 1910–65, the initial decline continues for six months and reaches 2.6 basis points. The ensuing rise in the interest rate takes

CHART 7-1

Lag Distribution of Monetary Effects on Commercial Paper Rate,
Various Periods, 1910–65

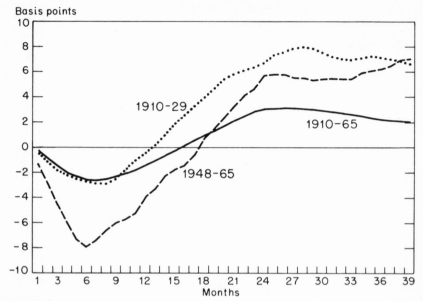

Note: Regression equation shown in text. Units are basis points per one percentage point change in annual rate of monetary growth (100 basis points = 1 percentage point of interest rate).

it past its starting level by the sixteenth month.[1] The coefficients and t
values are given in Table 7-1.

The other plots in Chart 7-1 show how the pattern differs between
the earlier and later subperiods. There is a smaller initial decline in the
earlier than in the later period, and a more rapid rise thereafter.[2] All
three curves reveal a strong positive effect still remaining after thirty-
nine months.

[1] Nineteen of the first 23 coefficients are significant at the .05 level in the full-period regression (see Table 7-1). None of the last 16 are. R is .37 and R^2 adjusted for degrees of
freedom is .08. A low correlation coefficient here should not be surprising, since the regression measures only one of the many influences on interest rates and is in first differences.

[2] An F test of differences between regression coefficients (not shown) for the 1910–42
and 1942–65 periods was not significant, however.

TABLE 7-1

Regression of Commercial Paper Rate on Lagged Values
of Monetary Growth Rate, First Differences of
Monthly Data, 1910–65

Regression Coefficients		t Values	Cumulative Sum of β Coefficients
Constant	2.20	0.03	
β_1	−0.35	−5.5	−0.35
β_2	−0.57	−6.8	−0.92
β_3	−0.60	−5.9	−1.52
β_4	−0.50	−4.5	−2.02
β_5	−0.33	−2.8	−2.35
β_6	−0.22	−1.8	−2.57
β_7	−0.06	−0.5	−2.63
β_8	0.07	0.6	−2.56
β_9	0.22	1.8	−2.34
β_{10}	0.28	2.3	−2.06
β_{11}	0.28	2.3	−1.78
β_{12}	0.34	2.8	−1.44
β_{13}	0.39	3.2	−1.05
β_{14}	0.37	3.0	−0.68
β_{15}	0.34	2.7	−0.34
β_{16}	0.43	3.5	+0.09
β_{17}	0.41	3.4	+0.50
β_{18}	0.37	3.0	+0.87
β_{19}	0.40	3.3	+1.27
β_{20}	0.41	3.3	+1.68
β_{21}	0.43	3.5	+2.11
β_{22}	0.38	3.1	+2.49
β_{23}	0.32	2.6	+2.81
β_{24}	0.19	1.5	+3.00
β_{25}	0.12	1.0	+3.12
β_{26}	0.06	0.5	+3.18
β_{27}	−0.01	−0.1	+3.17
β_{28}	−0.03	−0.2	+3.14
β_{29}	−0.07	−0.6	+3.07
β_{30}	−0.14	−1.2	+2.94
β_{31}	−0.11	−0.9	+2.83
β_{32}	−0.11	−0.9	+2.72

(continued)

TABLE 7-1 (concluded)

Regression Coefficients		t Values	Cumulative Sum of β Coefficients
β_{33}	−0.11	−1.0	+2.61
β_{34}	−0.09	−0.8	+2.52
β_{35}	−0.15	−1.3	+2.37
β_{36}	−0.14	−1.4	+2.23
β_{37}	−0.09	−0.9	+2.12
β_{38}	−0.05	−0.5	+2.07
β_{39}	−0.06	−1.0	+2.01

Note: For the form of the regression equation, see text equation. Units of the coefficients are basis points per one percentage point change in annual rate of change of money stock. $R = .367$. Adj. $R^2 = .081$.

Source: See the data appendix. Money is currency outside banks plus demand and time deposits.

With so many lagged terms, the problem of collinearity among the independent variables is a matter of concern. Here, however, only 109 of the 741 elements of the correlation matrix have values over 0.1, and the vast majority of these are under 0.2. That is one advantage of running the regression in first-difference form. Experimentation with various lengths of lag suggests that the point at which the pattern rises above zero is little affected by extending the lag beyond twenty months, nor is the position of the minimum point greatly affected. The lag with thirty-nine terms that is used in Chart 7-1 should therefore be long enough to give reliable estimates of at least the first part of the pattern.

It is important to emphasize that these lag patterns were not imposed upon the data in any way. The least-squares procedure minimizes the variance of the residual terms but does not constrain the regression coefficients. Yet the patterns generally conform to theoretical suppositions, showing first a decline and then a rise which carries the interest rate above its starting level.[3]

[3] Regressions (not shown) with bond yields and with Treasury bill rates for the post-World War II period have a shorter lag, in which the cumulative lag pattern crosses the zero line several quarters sooner than is shown here for the commercial paper rate. Similar results are reported by William Gibson, "The Lag in the Effect of Monetary Policy on Income and Interest Rates," *Quarterly Journal of Economics*, May 1970, pp.

The amplitude of the effect is small, however. During a typical business cycle, commercial paper rates can fluctuate over several hundred basis points. Monthly monetary growth fluctuates cyclically over a range of from perhaps five to ten percentage points at an annual rate, apart from any extreme rates for a short period. This would imply (according to the regression for the full period, which shows a maximum decline of 2.6 basis points) an effect on paper rates of at most 26 basis points, which is only a small part of their actual total fluctuation. As noted previously, this regression equation obviously explains only part of the cyclical fluctuation in interest rates.

A technical reason for the small amplitude of the estimated effect may be that the lag varies in length over the business cycle. Because the regression assumes a fixed lag, the estimated lag will be an average of the actual patterns. The maximum amplitude of the estimated pattern will then be less than a straight average of the maximum amplitudes of individual patterns.

Aside from reducing the amplitude of a changing lag, the estimated pattern does not in any direct way bias the average length. We may therefore take the estimates as a first approximation to the actual length. The Chart 7-1 patterns cross the zero line in 13 to 18 months. At the point of this crossover, the initial decline in the interest rate has been completely reversed. The rise in the pattern above zero thereafter can be attributed to the Fisher effect of anticipated inflation (which theoretically would eventually raise the interest rate 100 basis points above its original level).

We might expect the Fisher effect to show up more strongly after World War II, when prices were generally rising and expectations of inflation became widespread. Yet Chart 7-1 shows a lower pattern for the later than for the earlier period. This puzzling difference appears to reflect the behavior of time deposits. The rising interest rates following World War II tended to draw savings deposits from commercial banks

---

288–300, Table II. See also Gibson, "Interest Rates and Monetary Policy," *Journal of Political Economy,* May/June 1970.

Bond yields are much less responsive to short-run monetary effects than are short-term rates. And Treasury bill rates, compared with the commercial paper rate, are more volatile and more influenced by Federal Reserve and Treasury short-run supply changes. For these reasons the commercial paper rate has been used here for the analysis of lags.

to savings and loan associations because the associations paid a relatively more attractive return during most of the period, thanks in part to interest rate ceilings on time deposits at commercial banks, which were adjusted upward by the authorities with a lag. The associations had no ceilings until 1966 and could pay steadily more as their earnings (mostly on mortgages) rose. The money stock, including time deposits (as used in Chart 7-1), thus often grew less rapidly when interest rates were rising, which added to the inverse relationship produced by the effect of monetary growth on interest rates. As a result, the inverse relationship is stronger in the regression for the post-World War II

TABLE 7-2

Regression of Commercial Paper Rate on Lagged Monetary
Growth Rate, for Three Definitions of Money, Various
Post-World War II Periods, First Differences of
Quarterly Data, 1948–69

Lag Term in Months	Cumulative Sum of Lag Coefficients		
	Incl. Time Deposits, 1948–67	Incl. Time Deposits But Not CD's,[a] 1953–69	Excl. Time Deposits, 1953–65
$1\frac{1}{2}$	−8.7	−11.9	−7.0
$4\frac{1}{2}$	−11.0	−14.9	−3.0
$7\frac{1}{2}$	−9.8	−14.0	4.9
$10\frac{1}{2}$	−7.2	−11.9	12.9
$13\frac{1}{2}$	−4.5	−10.0	19.5
$16\frac{1}{2}$	−2.2	−8.5	24.8
$19\frac{1}{4}$	−0.5	−7.2	29.5
$22\frac{1}{2}$	0.8	−5.9	34.3
$25\frac{1}{2}$	1.2	−5.5	38.5
$28\frac{1}{2}$	0.5	−7.6	39.7
R^2	.44	.48	.57

Note: Lag distributions were fitted to a fifth-degree polynomial with no end-point constraints. Constant term is not shown. Coefficients are expressed in units of basis points per one percentage point change in annual rate of change of money stock.

[a] Large ($100,000 and over) negotiable certificates of deposit.

period, and this could delay the appearance of a positive lagged relationship due to the Fisher effect.

Table 7-2 presents some additional regressions for the post-World War II period which support this interpretation. These regressions use three different definitions of money and start and end in different years in order to avoid certain "problem" periods. The data are quarterly rather than monthly. To allow more degrees of freedom in the short periods covered, the lag terms were constrained to follow a polynomial distribution. The fitted distributions were of fifth degree with no constraints at either end, and with ten (quarterly) lag terms. The table gives the cumulative sum of the lag coefficients, which are dated in the middle of the quarter to which the sums apply; this form of presentation allows comparison with the monthly lag distributions shown in Chart 7-1. In all cases monetary growth is expressed as an annual percentage rate; so the units of measurement are comparable.

The lag pattern for the money stock including time deposits is approximately the same as that in Chart 7-1 for the later period. The small difference results from the two extra years covered here and the use of the polynomial distribution.

When time deposits are excluded altogether, the initial decline in the lag pattern is shorter and rises thereafter quite rapidly. In ten quarters it rises by four-tenths of the theoretical maximum of 100 basis points above zero. That points to a strong and rapid response of the Fisher effect. Indeed, it suggests a much more rapid response than has been found by other studies for earlier periods.

One component of time deposits exhibited a positive response to rising interest rates. Time certificates of deposit grew rapidly after 1960, particularly in the middle 1960's, when interest rates rose steeply. When large certificates of deposit are excluded from the money stock, the estimated lag pattern rises from its initial decline more slowly than in Chart 7-1 and fails to reach the zero line even after ten quarters. This confirms the importance in these estimates of the effect of interest rates on time deposits.

The effect of interest rates on time deposits helps to explain the different results among these regressions, but it does not imply which one gives the truest picture of economic behavior. To the extent (not easy to determine) that monetary policy offsets interest-rate effects on time deposits by keeping the growth of total deposits the same as it otherwise would have been, the wider definition is proper; and to the extent it does not, the narrow definition is proper. Also, to the extent that time deposits are substituted in the public's portfolios for demand deposits, the wider definition is proper. And to the extent that savings deposits in other institutions are substituted for time deposits, an even wider definition may be proper. These are unsettled issues.

There is another problem with the estimated rapid response of the Fisher effect in the regression for the narrow definition of money. The period covered was one of generally rising interest rates and prices. The increases in monetary growth which lie behind the price increases also tend to correlate positively, as the results show, with subsequent increases in interest rates. To attribute this correlation to the Fisher effect implies that the inflation was wholly responsible for the increase in interest rates. This overstates the Fisher effect to the extent that real rates of interest rose over this period. Certainly real rates of interest rose from the very low levels reached during the 1940's. They may have risen further during the subsequent period for a variety of reasons. The regression with the narrow money stock was terminated in 1965 to avoid the steep increases in interest rates in the years following, but this shortening of the period only partly circumvents the problem.

There are good reasons, therefore, for interpreting these results with caution and for not attributing the rapid rise in the pattern for the narrow money stock in Table 7-1 entirely to the Fisher effect. Yet, despite these imperfections, the equation with the narrow definition seems the most plausible of the three. After all, the economic climate of this period does suggest that the public was sensitive to inflation, and such sensitivity is consistent with a rising tail to the lag pattern.

The upshot of this discussion is that the post-World War II period does not give a clear picture of the lag pattern for *real* rates of interest. All the regressions conform to the general pattern implied by the portfolio and Fisher effects, but the full-period regression in Chart 7-1 probably gives the more reliable estimate. On that evidence short-term real rates of interest typically decline for two quarters following an increased rate of monetary growth, and then return to their original levels in about five quarters.

These results support the portfolio theory over the credit theory because the latter does not explain a return to the original level. Of course, a reformulated credit theory, in which the increased rate of monetary growth is deemed to have only a temporary effect, would be consistent with this evidence, as would a credit theory in combination with the Fisher effect. But given the relative importance of the portfolio effect found in Chapter 4, the initial part of the lag patterns estimated here should be attributed to portfolio adjustments.

THE LAGGED EFFECT ON AGGREGATE EXPENDITURES

In the Chapter 6 model of the portfolio effect, both aggregate expenditures and interest rates are affected by the portfolio adjustments set in motion by a monetary disturbance. The resulting movements in expenditures and interest rates are part of the same adjustment. The relation between aggregate expenditures and monetary growth therefore contains further evidence on the dynamic characteristics of the model.

In the theory, monetary growth affects income growth with a lag which is no longer, and may be shorter, than that for interest rates, though the two variables should reach a new long-run equilibrium at the same time. (Income and aggregate expenditures are considered to be the same here.) The income lag will be no longer because the return of interest rates to their original level requires corresponding changes in income. The income lag may be shorter because the effect of monetary growth on income growth involves overshooting, since the level of income first lags behind its long-run equilibrium relation with the money stock and then must grow faster than money for a time in order to catch up. A dependence of desired money balances on permanent income also contributes to overshooting (Appendix to Chapter 6). The income lag may also be shorter because a discrepancy between actual and desired money balances may be partly erased by direct expenditures on goods and services.

On the other hand, any credit effect on interest rates, though not likely to be permanent, can nonetheless continue on after the full effects on aggregate expenditures have been completed. A credit effect would tend to make the observed lag pattern for interest rates longer. In interpreting the results, we must also take account of the Fisher effect in speeding up the return time for interest rates. The return time for *real* rates of interest will be longer than the estimated time for nominal rates, though we cannot say by how much.

The relation between aggregate expenditures (represented by GNP or final sales) and monetary growth has been studied in a series of papers by the research staff of the Federal Reserve Bank of St. Louis and published in the bank's *Review*.[4] The regression presented in Table 7-3 reproduces the kind of equation they have publicized. It follows St. Louis in using the narrow definition of the money stock, which for this period gives the best fit among alternative definitions. The form of this regression, however, differs in certain respects from the "St. Louis equation." The variables in Table 7-3 are expressed as percentage rates of change rather than the change in dollar amounts; high-employment federal expenditures (the other independent variable used in the St. Louis equation) are excluded; and ten lag terms are included rather than only three or four. The purpose of including the extra terms here is to estimate the shape of the lag pattern over a fairly long period. The first of these differences affects the general shape of the pattern.[5] The use of dollar rather than percentage changes results in much less overshooting.

The estimated pattern indicates that monetary effects on aggregate expenditures are quite rapid. In Table 7-3 the cumulative effect reaches

---

[4] See Leonall C. Andersen and Jerry Jordan, "Monetary and Fiscal Actions: A Test of Their Relative Importance in Economic Stabilization," November 1968; and Michael W. Keran, "Monetary and Fiscal Influences on Economic Activity—The Historical Evidence," November 1969.

This work was undertaken to test the relative importance of monetary and fiscal influences on aggregate expenditures, following the earlier work of Friedman and Meiselman. Andersen and Jordan found the fiscal influence to be temporary and to contribute only modestly to the total correlation. The equation has subsequently been widely used for forecasting. In this respect it has clear limitations. R^2 in Table 7-3 is only .41. (As usually presented, with the variables expressed as changes in dollar amounts, R^2 is appreciably higher.) But the equation is certainly not bad, considering that it relies on only two time series for the independent variables.

[5] The positive constant term (1.06 per cent per quarter or 4.24 per cent per year) mainly represents the upward trend in GNP velocity over the period covered. The ratio of GNP to money stock over this period grew 3.5 per cent per year.

TABLE 7-3

Regression of Percentage Change in GNP on Lagged Values
of Monetary Growth Rate, Quarterly Data, 1953–69

Lag Term in Months	Regression Coefficients	t Values	Cumulative Sum of β Coefficients up to Last Significant Term
Constant	1.06	4.8	
$1\frac{1}{2}$	0.40	2.6	0.40
$4\frac{1}{2}$	0.43	5.5	0.83
$7\frac{1}{2}$	0.31	3.7	1.15
$10\frac{1}{2}$	0.14	2.2	1.28
$13\frac{1}{2}$	−0.02	−0.4	1.26
$16\frac{1}{2}$	−0.13	−1.8	1.13
$19\frac{1}{2}$	−0.16	−2.5	0.98
$22\frac{1}{2}$	−0.12	−1.8	
$25\frac{1}{2}$	−0.06	−0.7	
$28\frac{1}{2}$	−0.05	−0.6	
$31\frac{1}{2}$	−0.18	−1.0	

Note: Lagged coefficients are constrained by polynomial of fourth
degree with no end-point constraints. Money stock excludes time deposits. Units of coefficients are pure numbers; constant term, per cent
per quarter. $R^2 = .412$. GNP is published series from Department of
Commerce National Income Accounts.

unity six months after the initial change in monetary growth.[6] Unity is
the total long-run effect.[7] There is overshooting, however, and the
cumulative effect settles back close to unity by the eighteenth month,

[6] This seems surprisingly quick. It is usually contended that money has some effect
on business activity within six months, but it is seldom claimed that the maximum effect
occurs so quickly.

There may, however, be a statistical bias toward a shorter lag in these results because
of a dependence of monetary growth on concurrent changes in business activity. Andersen ("Additional Empirical Evidence on the Reserve-Causation Argument," Federal
Reserve Bank of St. Louis, *Review,* August 1969) shows that this dependence cannot account for the total correlation between aggregate expenditures and the lag in monetary growth, but the concurrent dependence is not shown to be zero and may spuriously
produce some shortening of the estimated lag.

[7] On the assumption that the income elasticity of demand for money balances is unity.

after which the lag terms are no longer statistically significant but suggest further small oscillations around the long-run equilibrium. Most published versions of the St. Louis equation are cut off after the third or fourth lag term. For this reason and also because those versions are expressed in dollar changes, where the theoretically complete effect is not obvious, the overshooting has not been emphasized.[8]

The eighteen months taken for the cumulative effect to settle back close to unity is an estimate of the minimum time to reach a new equilibrium. According to the Chapter 6 model, this time should coincide with the return of real interest rates to their original level. Commercial paper rates cross the zero line in seventeen months for the 1948–65 period in Chart 7-1, and the time would be longer if we could adjust for the upward pull of the Fisher effect. In Table 7-2 the number of months is greater for the two regressions including time deposits. These lag times are not inconsistent with the theoretical relationship. With time deposits excluded, the zero crossover is six months, far less than the return to unity for GNP of eighteen months in Table 7-2 (which also excludes time deposits), but the six-month interest-rate crossover is shortened considerably by a strong upward pull of the Fisher effect as indicated by the subsequent rise of the pattern.

We cannot be sure from these mixed results that the estimated lag patterns for commercial paper rates and GNP are fully consistent with the model of the portfolio effect in Chapter 6. Some of the patterns suggest a delay in the adjustment of interest rates relative to that for GNP which could be due to the credit effect, and some do not. But the general path of the adjustment process estimated here bears out the Chapter 6 model, though there is undoubtedly much room for its elaboration and improvement.

---

[8] Overshooting is nevertheless apparent in many of the published historical charts of the lag pattern. See especially Keran, "Monetary and Fiscal Influences," Chart II.

8

Summary and Implications

TWO TRADITIONS IN MONETARY THEORY

The double function of commercial banks—they both create money and make loans—has had considerable influence on the development of monetary theory. One example is the confusion that long existed over the expansion of deposits. Bankers used to deny that they created deposits: from their point of view, deposits created by expanding loans were withdrawn by the borrowers and disappeared from the books of the lending bank. The question was finally resolved by drawing a distinction between individual banks and the banking system, as is now commonplace in money and banking textbooks.

The double function of commercial banks also lies behind the uneasy coexistence of two approaches to monetary theory and policy. One, the quantity-theory tradition, emphasizes the supply of and demand for the stock of money. The other, a credit theory of money, emphasizes the effect of banks on the supply of loanable funds. The two approaches are not theoretically incompatible. They fit together consistently in a general description of long-run equilibrium. In the analysis of changes in the money stock and credit, however, they give rise to different and often opposing interpretations.

The quantity-theory tradition focuses on the adjustments of the public to a change in money balances. Portfolio theory, which describes the allocation of tangible wealth among various alternative assets, is the modern development of this tradition. The adjustments in portfolios to a monetary change ultimately affect all dollar values in the economy but initially have important effects also on interest rates.

The portfolios of banks are also disturbed by a monetary change, but in this tradition the particular financial assets acquired by banks in expanding deposits are not important in determining the amount and the speed of the effect on aggregate expenditures.

For credit theories, however, the credit flows emanating from banks and other financial institutions are of prime importance. In this view the speed and direction of monetary effects depend upon the manner in which new money enters the economy. In one version of the credit effect, attributable to Wicksell, an expansion of bank credit adds to the total supply of real loanable funds and thus reduces interest rates, while by implication an expansion of the money stock by other means does not. It is sometimes argued further that monetary expansion affects aggregate expenditures more rapidly and more predictably if banks expand loans rather than investments. The rationale is that, since purchases of existing securities change only the composition of the public's portfolios, the effect on expenditures is slow and uncertain, while loans put money into the hands of households and businessmen who intend to spend it immediately.

The quantity and credit theories often lie behind differing approaches to monetary policy. A recent example was the "bills only" controversy of the early 1960's, in which the issue was whether the Federal Reserve should conduct open-market operations in long-term bonds rather than in Treasury bills, as was usual. The opponents of "bills only" followed a credit-theory approach. They argued that operating in bonds would more directly affect long-term interest rates. Allegedly, investment expenditures would respond more quickly. Then open-market operations would have a speedier and greater impact on aggregate expenditures. This argument emphasizes the first-round effects of changes in the money stock.[1] The quantity-theory tradition, on the other hand, attaches little importance to the first-round effects. By implication, the Federal Reserve's choice of securities to buy or sell has little impact on aggregate expenditures.

Another example of the influence of credit theories is the long-

---

[1] There would, of course, be further effects in the first round as banks expanded or contracted in response to the change in bank reserves. The way in which banks respond is largely beyond the control of the Federal Reserve, however, and was disregarded in the "bills only" discussion.

standing reliance on particular "credit market conditions" to indicate the immediate effects of monetary policy. These conditions include money market interest rates as well as the terms and availability of credit in major financial markets. One rationale given for this emphasis is that the main channels of monetary effects on the economy are the credit flows through financial institutions. In the quantity-theory approach, however, interest rates and other credit conditions are only one channel of monetary effects. The portfolio adjustments set in motion by a change in money balances can work through a variety of channels rather than exclusively through the credit flows of financial institutions. Portfolio adjustments also affect credit markets, as one among various sectors, but not in the narrow sense of always having a particular impact.

THEORETICAL ANALYSIS OF THE CREDIT EFFECT

These two approaches to monetary theory and policy imply a different pattern of monetary effects on interest rates, though the differences between the two are often blurred in the literature. The differences are emphasized in the present study so that their separate roles in monetary disturbances can be tested.

The starting point is a theoretical analysis, in Chapter 2, of an important proposition underlying most credit theories, namely, that an expansion of bank credit adds to the total supply of real loanable funds and therefore affects real saving in the economy. The explanation usually given is that the operating procedures of financial institutions produce "forced" saving, overriding household preferences which determine the desired additions to wealth.

An alternative is to view bank credit expansion as the revenue from creating money, and to ask what determines the amount of the revenue in real terms and whether its beneficiaries increase their saving rather than their consumption. The analysis of the first part of Chapter 2 leads to the conclusion that lack of free entry into banking and of full competition in attracting depositors allows deposit expansion to produce a revenue. Yet institutional practices do not require that it produce increased real saving in the economy. If the beneficiaries of the revenue, the banks' stockholders, view the revenue as income, they will probably want to consume most of it—not save it. They can control their total saving even if the revenue is not paid to them as dividends but is retained by the banks.

Nevertheless, it is likely that stockholders will save unanticipated increases in the revenue from deposit expansion. Consequently, unanticipated short-run variations in deposit growth may tend to produce some corresponding variations in the supply of real loanable funds and opposite variations in interest rates, while long-run anticipated rates of growth will tend not to.

STATISTICAL ANALYSIS OF THE EFFECTS

A 1966 study of mine found that the U.S. data do in fact show an inverse association between interest rates and the rate of growth of the money stock. A modified version of that work was presented here in Chapter 3. The association raises an important question for monetary theory: "Does the association reflect the credit or the portfolio effect or in part both?" The only other plausible explanation of the association is the reverse effect of interest rates on monetary growth, but this alternative was examined and found to be untenable. It would most likely produce a positive association, if any at all.

In Chapters 4 and 5, a statistical analysis was developed to test the portfolio and credit theories by the implied effects on interest rates. Interest rates were regressed on two variables representing two sources of monetary growth. One source was monetary growth associated with credit expansion of the monetary system. (Treasury debt operations can be either consolidated with Federal Reserve Bank operations or excluded, depending upon how broadly the "monetary system" is defined. The analysis alternately used both definitions.) The second source was all other components of monetary growth—those not associated with credit expansion of the monetary system, such as gold flows and Treasury budget deficits financed by creating money. The regression of interest rates on the two main sources of monetary growth indicated the extent to which each one accounted for the inverse association. By the credit theory the first source would account for all of the inverse association with interest rates, and the second source for none. By the portfolio theory both sources would account equally for the association, since all sources of monetary growth are supposed to affect interest rates.

The results showed that the portfolio effect accounts for most or all of the association. The credit effect measured separately was usually not statistically significant, whereas the portfolio effect uniformly was.

Various estimates of the regression coefficient of the credit variable consistently suggest that its additional effect is not zero, however, even though most of the individual estimates are not statistically significant. Taken all together, these estimates provide tentative evidence that the credit effect has an independent existence. According to the estimates, new money has a greater *initial* effect on interest rates, if it enters the economy through an expansion of credit, of about 10 to 40 or 50 per cent. Additional analysis suggests that Federal Reserve credit by itself may account for much of this effect. A larger effect for Federal Reserve credit than for bank credit is consistent with the theoretical proposition that credit expansion by the government is not offset by the public, whereas that of commercial banks is to some extent offset by stockholders or depositors.

The credit effect, therefore, is considerably smaller than the portfolio effect for the intermediate-run periods tested here, and for longer periods the credit effect is presumably even smaller. The first-round effects of money creation associated with an expansion of credit are but the tip of an iceberg. The initial impact on particular financial markets is outweighed by the subsequent rounds of portfolio adjustments. Monetary growth produces an effect on interest rates no matter how the new money is created. The effects are therefore not confined to particular markets but range widely throughout the economy.

THE SEQUENCE OF MONETARY EFFECTS ON INTEREST RATES

The portfolio effect can be interpreted as a gradual adjustment to a discrepancy between actual and desired money balances. This process was analyzed theoretically in Chapter 6 and statistically in Chapter 7, and can explain most of the inverse association between interest rates and monetary growth.

The effect is not permanent. The discrepancy leads to adjustments involving purchases and sales of financial and real assets which affect aggregate expenditures and thus the amount of money balances demanded. The effect on money demand tends to erase the discrepancy and thus to bring real interest rates back to their initial level. Nominal interest rates continue to adjust, however, presumably until they fully compensate for the anticipated rate of price change.

According to the model of the portfolio effect developed in Chapter 6, monetary effects on interest rates are accompanied by a corresponding sequence of effects on aggregate expenditures. Following a monetary disturbance, interest rates initially respond inversely to the disturbance, but later reverse direction and return to their original level. The turnabout and return take place because aggregate expenditures are also responding to the disturbance. This response reflects an effect on borrowing for investment expenditures and on direct expenditures for goods as part of the adjustment of portfolios. The model therefore provides a rationale for equations of the St. Louis type, which relate changes in aggregate expenditures to current and lagged monetary growth.

Statistical analysis of the lag pattern supports the sequence implied by the model. The pattern for the commercial paper rate shows an initial inverse movement and subsequent reversal. The return movement goes further than the initial level, apparently reflecting the Fisher effect of the anticipated rate of price change. The lagged effect on aggregate expenditures exhibits overshooting, which in the model is due to an initial change in the ratio of money to income followed by a return to the equilibrium level. Overshooting is greater if desired money balances depend upon permanent rather than current income.

These lag patterns are crucial for the proper conduct of monetary policy. An emphasis on the credit effects of monetary policy has tended to foster the view that its effects occur relatively quickly, whereas the portfolio effects are consistent with a delayed adjustment and lags in monetary policy. The estimates suggest that the initial inverse effect lasts one to two quarters or so, and that interest rates then reverse direction and pass their original levels in three to five quarters. Overshooting in the accompanying adjustment of aggregate expenditures obviously adds to the difficulties of monetary policy in varying monetary growth to stabilize the economy.

SOME IMPLICATIONS FOR POLICY
FORECASTS AND INDICATORS

Econometric Models

In many econometric models of the economy, monetary effects are measured indirectly by means of interest-rate variables. Interest rates enter into asset demand, credit demand, and supply equations for these markets. The money stock influences interest rates through the demand function for money balances, and interest rates in turn influence investment expenditures. A common criticism of these models is that the small number of quoted interest rates covered may not represent the full range of portfolio adjustments. Also, quoted rates may not reveal the "true" cost or return to lending along certain channels, and those rates may not adequately represent the variety of channels through which changes in borrowing and expenditures occur. In consequence, monetary effects on aggregate expenditures may be understated.

One can sidestep the statistical problem of coverage by incorporating monetary adjustments directly into the equations. One procedure is to put the discrepancy between actual and desired money balances into the expenditure equations. That is highly dependent upon an accurate estimate of desired money balances, however, and is not likely to be successful. An alternative is illustrated by the solution to the simplified model of Chapter 6. This relates expenditures to current and past rates of change in the money stock. The inclusion of lagged monetary growth in expenditure equations may help to catch monetary effects not adequately represented by interest rates and by approximations to the terms and availability of credit.

The rationale for making expenditures depend upon monetary growth rather than the growth of a broader set of financial assets is that monetary growth largely occurs independently of the portfolio decisions of the public. There are, to be sure, unsettled questions about how exogenous to the economic system the various components of the money stock are. But, generally speaking, the reserves and demand deposits of commercial banks change independently of immediate market developments. Nowadays excess reserves remain at minimum working amounts, and the Federal Reserve does not, most of the time, allow borrowed reserves to influence for long the level of total reserves intended by policy. Consequently, the exogenous supply factors largely determine the quantity of deposits outstanding, and currency outstanding grows steadily and does not produce important variations in growth of the total money stock. Portfolios then adjust to changes in the supply of money. Other financial assets, on the other hand, cannot be issued as a medium of exchange, but are created by inducing someone to acquire them. A change in their rate of growth does not carry the same significance for expenditures as does a change in monetary growth.

Another characteristic of many econometric models concerns their treatment of monetary effects on interest rates. These effects are most often explained in terms of a demand function for money balances dependent upon the level of interest rates and aggregate expenditures. (Dollar magnitudes should theoretically be in real terms, but are often measured in nominal terms.) It is generally assumed in the models that portfolio adjustments are rapid, so that actual and desired money balances can be taken as always equal. Then the equation, simultaneously with the rest of the model, helps determine the level of interest rates.

As a method of estimation this differs radically from the regressions reported in Chapter 7 between the level of interest rates and past *rates of change* of the money stock. The derivation of the equations is also different. The model of Chapter 6 described monetary effects on interest rates in terms of a discrepancy between desired and actual money balances. On the assumption that portfolio adjustments take time, discrepancies reflect past changes in the rate of change of the money stock.

Despite the dissimilarity of the estimation methods, they can be given a common interpretation. In the Chapter 6 model, desired money balances were represented as a function of the interest rate and aggregate expenditures. This function can be substituted for desired money balances in the equation relating the interest rate to the discrepancy between actual and desired balances. When solved for the interest rate, this gives a relation between the interest rate, the money stock, and aggregate expenditures — the same way as in the econometric models described above. While the method of Chapter 6 estimates the discrepancy between actual and desired money balances from changes in

monetary growth, the econometric models can be interpreted as measuring the discrepancy directly by the use of actual money balances
and an estimate of desired balances, the latter based on predicted
values of aggregate expenditures derived from the whole model.
Hence the difference between these estimation methods is in the appli-
cation rather than the basic theory, though the interpretation of regression coefficients will be different.

An interest-rate equation using aggregate expenditures as a proxy for
desired money balances gives a good fit, in large part because it accounts well for long-run movements in the variables. But this does not
mean that it properly describes short-run movements in interest rates.
Actually, such an equation in first-difference form does poorly. Small
errors in estimates of desired money balances by this method can produce large percentage errors in the discrepancy between actual and
desired balances, as was noted earlier. The accuracy of this method of
explaining interest rates and that of Chapters 6 and 7, which is based
on past rates of monetary growth, cannot be properly assessed from
correlation coefficients but only from *ex ante* predictions, when the
monetary growth path alone is assumed to be known. Then the two are
on an equal footing, and such a comparison of their comparative pre-
dictive powers would provide a further test of the Chapter 6 model.

These models can only be of value in explaining short-run changes in
interest rates, since monetary changes will have no long-run effects on
real rates of interest.

Compartmentalized Financial Markets

The importance of credit effects is commonly thought to derive from
separate "compartments" in financial markets, whereby credit channeled into particular markets cannot easily "escape" to take advantage of more attractive returns elsewhere. It is alleged, for example,
that a rapid rise in interest rates hampers a free flow of funds into the
mortgage market because of institutional restraints. Policies to divert
funds into the mortgage market and elsewhere have therefore been pursued in times of monetary restraint, on the assumption that if funds are
channeled there the market receives largely the same supply from other
sources and ends up with a larger total supply.

The results of this study do not deny the existence of institutional restraints over the flow of funds into particular financial markets. Legal constraints, risk of default, and investment policies of financial institutions, along with elasticities of demand, undoubtedly affect certain interest rate differentials and the quantity of funds supplied for particular purposes, though it does not follow that all funds supplied to an allegedly compartmentalized market are unable to flow elsewhere.

The findings of this study nevertheless bear on this issue, because they show that the first-round effects of monetary policy are a fairly small part of the total effect, whether the recipient markets are compartmentalized or not. It was also found that loans and investments of the banking system have little differential effect on loan rates and security yields. Most of the total effect on credit depends upon portfolio adjustments in subsequent rounds, which spread out into a variety of channels over which the initial lender has no control. These adjustments will outlast and swamp any initial credit effects of money creation on interest rates and aggregate expenditures. This means that bank credit is basically a poor guide to the effects that a particular monetary policy will have on the economy. Indeed, the main conclusion of this study is that monetary effects on interest rates and the economy at large depend primarily upon the quantity of money created and not upon the particular credit channels taken by the injection of new money.

Data Sources

MONEY, EARNING ASSETS, AND U.S. DEBT

Money supply and determinants (currency outside banks plus demand and time deposits of all commercial banks unless otherwise noted; high-powered money, reserve ratio, and currency ratio as defined in source): Milton Friedman and Anna J. Schwartz, *A Monetary History of the United States,* New York, NBER, 1963, appendix tables, revised and extended by data from *Federal Reserve Bulletin.* See also Friedman and Schwartz, *Monetary Statistics of the United States,* New York, NBER, 1970. Revised data in *Federal Reserve Bulletin,* December 1970, for 1967–69 expansion in Chart 3-1.

Treasury deposits in commercial banks: *ibid.*

Earning assets (loans and investments of weekly reporting member banks or all commercial banks plus Federal Reserve credit outstanding exclusive of loans to banks): *Banking and Monetary Statistics* and *Federal Reserve Bulletin,* both issued by the Board of Governors of the Federal Reserve System.

U.S. debt (interest-bearing federal debt outside U.S. agencies and Federal Reserve banks, end of month): NBER compilation to 1939, and *Monthly Treasury Bulletin* thereafter.

All monthly data are seasonally adjusted. Annual changes are based on June figures.

INTEREST RATES

Commercial paper: February 1936 and after computed from weekly data in *Commercial and Financial Chronicle;* January 1868–January 1936, from Frederick R. Macaulay, *Some Theoretical Problems Sug-*

gested by the Movements of Interest Rates, Bond Yields and Stock Prices in the United States since 1856, New York, NBER, 1938. Seasonally adjusted except 1927–52.

Treasury bills (Treasury notes and certificates to 1929, bills thereafter): *Federal Reserve Bulletin.* Seasonally adjusted except 1931–47.

Bank loans: First quarter 1939 and after, *Federal Reserve Bulletin;* January 1928–December 1938, unpublished data supplied by Board of Governors of the Federal Reserve System; January 1919–December 1927, *Banking and Monetary Statistics.*

High-grade corporate and municipal bonds, January 1900 and after: Simple average of municipal, railroad, public utility, and industrial bond yields from Standard & Poor's Corporation, *Security Price Index Record.* Not seasonally adjusted.

Long-term U.S. bonds: *Federal Reserve Bulletin.* Seasonally adjusted 1948–61 only.

Low-grade corporate bonds (Baa): Moody's Investors Service, *Industrial Manual.* Seasonally adjusted 1948–61 only.

High-grade railroad bonds: January, 1873–December, 1914, Macaulay, *Some Theoretical Problems.* Not seasonally adjusted.

Annual changes are based on fiscal-year averages of monthly figures.

Index